MY LIFE IN SCHOOL

Tom Stohl

Published by Public Schools of Tomorrow
Scarsdale, New York

Printed in the United States of America.

ISBN (PAPERBACK): 1493763326
ISBN 13 (PAPERBACK): 978-1-4937633-2-0
ISBN (HARDCOVER): 978-0-983470
ISBN 13 (HARDCOVER): 978-0-9834703-5-9
Library of Congress Control Number: 2012922326

Design: Nieto Books, Brooklyn
Cover photograph courtesy of the New York Department of Education.

This book is dedicated to

DR. GIBRAN MAJDALANY
TEACHERS COLLEGE
COLUMBIA UNIVERSITY

A true and valued friend whose intellectual, spiritual, and physical
strength made it possible for me to work in a challenging time.

CONTENTS

Foreword *ix*

Preface *xiii*

Introduction *3*

CHAPTER ONE: Beginnings *13*

CHAPTER TWO: Schooling *37*

CHAPTER THREE: Korea *51*

CHAPTER FOUR: Teacher *63*

CHAPTER FIVE: Scarsdale *85*

CHAPTER SIX: Albany *111*

CHAPTER SEVEN: Teachers College, Columbia University *143*

Epilogue *183*

Notes *185*

Appendix *189*

Acknowledgments *223*

FOREWORD

Fifty-one years ago, Tom Sobol and I were new faculty members at Fox Lane High School in Mount Kisco, New York: I, a brand new business education teacher, and Tom, the new head of English, following his several years in army intelligence and teaching in Newton, Massachusetts. Little did I know, however, of the profound impact that this man would have on my own outlook on leadership, which I ultimately carried forward into a thirty-five-year career as a school superintendent in four states.

Tom had a teaching assignment of two English classes in addition to his leadership responsibilities, and he purposefully did not take the "Honors" classes but rather, classes filled with students for whom literature and grammar were a chore that they viewed as meaningless to their own lives. Many of those students were also in my classes, eager to develop a marketable skill that would get them a job during and after high school. With these students in common, Tom and I frequently fell into conversations about how to help these adolescents maximize what we saw as a lot of latent talent and skill sets. I quickly noticed that Tom avoided the faculty lounge as much as I did; both of us were turned off by the all-too-often negative staff conversations about individual students or about the administration. We found other venues to talk and compare our successes and our failures with individual students, who we really wanted to succeed as learners.

Ultimately, Tom and I both ended up in assignments in the school district's central office. It was a time of significant political turmoil in the district, with multiple changes in administration. One seminal event stands out in my mind: we were both so upset with the direction and tone of leadership that it was noticed by the board president who invited us to his home one evening to talk about our concerns. We decided in advance that we had to "tell it like it is," even if the consequences meant we couldn't remain with the district. The board president, a bright, thoughtful New York City business executive, assured us of his understanding and support when he said: "Our job as leaders is to place the flag at the top of the pole (we advocate for what is the very best); if others bring the flag down lower, it will be at their hand." We were reassured, there was a course correction in the district, and we moved positively forward.

As I read this memoir and call to action from a brilliant, highly skilled, and ethical leader, I was struck by how many times a vignette revealed Tom's courage and ability to inspire others while "putting the flag at the top of the pole":

- In his home with his brothers and parents
- In his military experiences
- In his teaching—of children, their parents, their community, and their political leaders
- In his work and conversations with young people
- In his cultural sensitivity to students, community, and staff
- In his political and policy decision-making and writings as commissioner
- In his scholarship and teaching at the university.

Tom's incredible sensitivity to doing what is "best," and not necessarily "politic," is probably best symbolized for me in an obscure assignment we had for the dedication of the newly constructed middle school in Mount Kisco. The Ford Foundation had provided significant financial assistance to the district to allow the district to be one of the first in the nation (early 1960s) to plan a new middle school facility around a well-articulated middle school philosophy. A "Committee of 100 Citizens" spearheaded the planning.

Our assignment was to recommend the wording for the dedicatory bronze plaque that would be prominently displayed in the lobby of the central building of this award-winning facility. Many ideas had been provided to us as to whom the building should be dedicated: "the Ford Foundation for its insight and generosity," or "the members of the school board for their far-sighted leadership," or "the Committee of 100 for its philosophical vision," or "the staff and administration for designing the groundbreaking middle school philosophy and program," etc. After a period of silence and reflection, Tom said, "No! None of the above. Those people have been or will be recognized in one way or another, but they are not the persons to whom the building should be dedicated."

Below, then, is the plaque that remains on the wall of that middle school fifty years later: This school is dedicated to each pupil who enters...that each may discover his own talent for learning, for growth and for service.

I think that you'll enjoy this book (which Tom typed with one finger while confined to his bed), because it's full of stories, hope, and humor. We still have so much to learn from the dedicated, ethical, caring, and articulate educator and leader, Tom Sobol.

—Charles Fowler

PREFACE

I have been attending and working in schools for most of my life. Except for three years in the U.S. Army, I have been either a student, a teacher, a school superintendent, a state education commissioner, or a college professor every day since September 1936, when I first walked into my neighborhood kindergarten and let go of my mother's hand. That's almost eighty years. I am astonished to have lived so long. As Casey Stengel used to say in his later years, "Most men my age are dead." How may I redeem the time? I must have learned something useful. I would like to share it with you. This memoir will tell you—students, teachers, parents, academics, policy makers, interested citizens—what has and hasn't worked as I've tried to improve education in several complex arenas. I offer you a distillation of lessons learned during many years of reflective practice.

The memoir contains two stories: my personal story and my professional story. My personal story is that of a working-class child who becomes a teacher and rises to some eminence. The early chapters describe the people and events that shaped me growing up. My professional story describes the educational issues and activities with which I was engaged. These discussions dominate the second part of the book. However, the personal is so intertwined with the professional that they cannot be clearly separated. Two stories, but one life: one book. You can't have one without the other.

A final word: I have not written a treatise. This book is not a research study, not an academic argument concerning education ideologies, or a recipe for curing whatever ills assail us. It is one man's subjective, imperfect, but honest effort to lay open the substance of his lifetime of professional experience, hoping that you will find a thing or two that raises a useful question.

INTRODUCTION

Let me begin in the middle of things, with a defining moment of my life, a vantage point from which we can look both backward and forward: it was a Sunday. The aroma of baking bread filled the house. I had put the loaves in the oven before sitting down at my desk. My writing tools, a yellow lined pad and several sharpened pencils, sat in front of me. It was the sixteenth Labor Day weekend on which I needed to write a speech welcoming teachers back to school. I wanted it to be a speech of hope that would reaffirm the importance of their work. If I could finish the speech in time, I could go to the Goldbergs' annual Labor Day barbecue.

In January I would be fifty-five years old. I had been Scarsdale superintendent of schools for almost sixteen years. They were wonderful years, but sixteen years was a long time: sixteen school budgets, sixteen speeches to teachers, hundreds of board of education meetings, and who knows how many snowy mornings when I had to decide at 4:00 a.m. whether to close the schools, knowing that the snow might stop at any time, and the streets might be cleared by early morning. "One more big job," I had said to Harriet many times. "I want one more big job." She would nod her head, but I could feel her tension. Change was difficult for her, and a new job for me would be a big change for her. For all the years she knew me, I had been superintendent of schools in Scarsdale.

Some months later, Gordon Ambach, NYS commissioner of education, announced he would be leaving the coming summer. As soon as I heard, I applied for the position. What I didn't know was that, though the Board of Regents were interviewing me, they had already promised members of the legislature's Black and Puerto Rican Caucus that they would appoint a person of color to be the new commissioner. And that is precisely what they did.

My heart sank when I heard the news. The interviews had gone well, and I thought I had a good chance at the job. But the regents had offered the position to Bernard Gifford, a highly regarded black man then serving as education dean at Berkeley, but previously a deputy superintendent in New York City—obviously a good choice.

The next day Marty Barell, chancellor of the Board of Regents, called me. Bernie Gifford had decided to stay at Berkeley.

Chancellor Barell asked, "Do you want the job?"

"Yes," I answered.

On March 24, 1987, the New York State Board of Regents voted fifteen-to-one that I be appointed commissioner of education. I was elated.

The day after the regents' vote, the protests from members of the caucus began. They were irate. Chancellor Barell, Deputy Chancellor Carballada, and other Regents received angry phone calls from the caucus members, arguing that they had been betrayed. I wasn't qualified, they said. How could I possibly be able to educate their kids? They didn't need a white man from Scarsdale as commissioner. The regents had broken their promise.

Perhaps, some of the caucus leaders said, the legislature should strip the regents of their powers.

They wanted me out. They wanted my appointment revoked. Chancellor Barell explained to the caucus members that the charge of "not keeping their word" was a misunderstanding. Barell and Carballada acknowledged that their ultimate choice was not a person of color, but their offer of the position to Dr. Gifford was proof of their good intentions.

Nevertheless, the caucus wanted me out. Immediately.

I was not surprised by their anger, but the intensity was unexpected. Although I hadn't known about the promise the regents had made, I knew of the anger many African-American people felt. During my first few months as Scarsdale superintendent, I had been confronted with disdain by Kenneth Clark, a respected African-American scholar. At a public meeting in Westchester County, Dr. Clark dismissed me as a privileged white man from Harvard who knew nothing about educating poor children. The attack was devastating. I could only express my respect for his work with the Supreme Court case, *Brown v. the Board of Education*.

Race, identity, and culture were center stage in the educational debate. Black and Hispanic intellectuals were asking why so many of their kids were failing. Were our schools at fault? Many believed that their contribution to our nation had been neglected in our history books. Consequently there was little with which their kids could identify. Students and professors at universities were protesting the lack of black and Hispanic faculty. Black history classes had been established in some high schools and colleges, but not enough, said their promoters. In the March 25, 1987 edition of *The New York Times*, an article announcing my appointment stated, "Dr. Sobol's election comes while the regents have been widely criticized for what has been called an insensitivity to the needs of so-called at-risk children, largely poor and urban minority-group members who are more likely than others to drop out." It was easy to understand why caucus members were angry at my appointment. The story of the Scarsdale superintendent and the righteous legislators didn't die quickly. Most of the press, with its thirst for controversy, seized the matter and began milking it dry. News media throughout the state reported the story of the regents' appointment of the elitist Scarsdalian, and prolonged it with editorials and commentary.

Many school practitioners, on the other hand, were delighted with the appointment. I knew what their jobs were and I respected the work they did. School people knew me and considered me approachable. There had never been a career school practitioner appointed to the post of commissioner of education.

Into the fray stepped Mario Cuomo, then governor of New York. Understand that in New York the governor and the commissioner of education have no direct reporting relationship with each other. The commissioner is chosen by, and reports to, the Board of Regents, which is in turn elected by the legislature. The governor is excluded from this part of the formal education decision-making process, an arrangement unloved by all New York state governors over time. The potential for conflict is inevitable. Nonetheless, the governor has other great powers, including determining the budget and, of course, the bully pulpit. Looking forward to meeting someone I had long admired, I went to Albany at his request.

We spent the better part of an hour in his office talking. First, two of his aides sat in, but after a while it was just the governor and me. We had a pleasant conversation. I was impressed by him and by his grasp of the issues. When our conversation ended, we went out of his office through a side door into a room where about two dozen members of the press sat waiting for us. I sat beside the governor at a table with two chairs facing the crowd.

"Governor, how do you feel about a commissioner who comes from the suburbs at a time when our cities are going down the tubes?" a reporter called out. Without giving the governor a chance to answer the question, someone from the back of the room asked, "Mr. Sobol, what do you have to say to people who say there is nothing in your Scarsdale experience—forgive me, sir—that could possibly qualify you for..." I opened my mouth to answer when the governor, without in any way putting me down, leaned forward across the table and put his hand on my arm. The reporters quieted down and waited for the governor to speak.

Governor Mario Cuomo and Tom at Tom's inauguration, 1987. Courtesy of the New York State Department of Education.

He folded his hands on the table and looked straight at the cluster of reporters. He told them to write the story any way they wanted to, but he and I were not going to play that game. He added that there was no question in his mind that my agenda was predominantly the same as his, and his was the Black Caucus's agenda. The reporters were busy writing down what the Governor was saying. He continued to speak, saying that he believed that I had a keen awareness of the special need to deal with disadvantaged students.

A reporter in the front looked at me. "Mr. Sobol, members of the Black and Puerto Rican Legislative Caucus have called you insensitive to affirmative action, insensitive to minorities, and even insensitive to middle income people. Do you have an answer for them?"

"Yes, sir," I responded. "I don't blame black and Hispanic legislators for feeling I am insensitive to minority needs. I understand their anxiety. It comes from generations of injustice. But they don't know me. I am confident that the deeds that will come from the commissioner's office will be reassuring to them."

Cuomo ended the press conference by telling the reporters that he and I had just had a pleasant conversation and he was impressed by what he heard. He added that the reporters didn't know me and he didn't know me yet either. But, he said, he was going to give me a chance. He urged them to do the same. "Thank you, governor," I said. "You are correct. They don't know me. Yes, I am white and yes, I am a Harvard graduate, and yes I worked and live in Scarsdale. But there is more."

Later that day, as I drove home, I knew that I would never forget the decency and kindness of Governor Cuomo's gesture of support. He stuck his neck out to help me, knowing that he had nothing to gain and could only get in trouble by defending me, if things didn't work out. The whole episode was exhilarating.

A day or two later a reporter asked me how I felt about being rated second to Bernie Gifford. I managed a grin and said, "I don't mind playing Lou Gehrig to Bernie Gifford's Babe Ruth."

I was appointed to the position in March, but was not scheduled to begin work until July. However, the problem of race was not a matter to postpone. While still fulfilling my obligations to Scarsdale, I began work at once with the State Education Department, meeting first with the caucus itself, then with minority groups throughout the state, listening to people's concerns and aspirations. The meetings were not only informative, they were cathartic. Participants talked openly and seemed pleased that someone was listening.

From these discussions, participants and I identified four problems/opportunities for immediate attention: high school dropouts, overrepresentation of black males in special education classes, underrepresentation of minorities on State Education Department staff, and the state's curriculum guides concerning minority people. Once I was in Albany, I appointed four committees (one for each priority area), charged them, provided staff, and turned them loose. Three committees submitted helpful findings and recommendations that led to positive change. So did the fourth committee, but it was soon clear that on this matter, we had a tiger by the tail.

Like the first three, the fourth committee consisted chiefly of minorities—a college president, three university professors, two superintendents of schools, a respected physician, and the state chairperson of the NAACP, as well as other educators and child advocates. This committee went about its task with diligence and passion. But if you ask a group of people what they think about a sensitive issue, they are apt to tell you how they feel as well. And there were some very strong feelings. Some months later I received the task force's report, entitled *A Curriculum of Inclusion*.

The report was scathing. The executive summary stated that "African Americans, Asian Americans, Puerto Ricans/Latinos, and Native Americans have been the victims of an intellectual and educational oppression that has characterized the culture and institutions of the United States

and the European American world for centuries....Task force members...
found that the current New York State Education Department curriculum materials...are contributing to the miseducation of all young people
through a systematic bias toward European culture and its derivatives."[1]

The task force made nine recommendations to accomplish what it saw
as necessary reforms in the state's curriculum, ranging from a revision of
curricular materials to teacher education and school administrator programs. Now the ball was in my court. What should I do with the report and
its recommendations?

The education commissioner's office in Albany contains a large and or-
nate beamed ceiling, a tiled fireplace, rich furnishings, and oil paintings on
the walls. I had met with the co-chairs of the task force and was now in my
office with my two chief deputies, Skip Meno and Sam Walton. What were
we to do with this report? Should we submit it to the Board of Regents, and
thereby to the press, at a public meeting? Or should we thank the committee, and quietly bury the report in the files, at least for now?

Skip, who is white, spoke first. "Don't do it. If that report gets out you
will have to accept it or reject it, and either way we'll be hearing from the
legislature forever. You came up here with a new agenda for poor kids, and
we're making a good start. This will kill the whole thing. We'll never get
the money we need from the legislature. Tom, if you have any sense, put
this distraction aside."

Sam, who is black, spoke next. "Skip may be right. I think he probably
is. But you know what, Tom? I never thought I'd be in a room like this,
much less work there. And here's a chance to speak the truth in policy-
making circles. I may never again have a chance like this. Tom, if you have
any courage, accept the report in public and live with the consequences."

I accepted the report and gave it to the regents at a public meeting,
endorsing its gist but not all its recommendations. Skip was right—all
hell broke loose. Over a period of months, perhaps longer, the national
press castigated me for "Africanizing" the curriculum, rewriting history

to make minorities feel good, and pandering to extremist black groups. Al Shanker, the president of the American Federation of Teachers, devoted at least six of his columns to our folly. *The New Republic* did a piece on "Sobol's Planet." A *New York Post* editorial, "Sobol's War on Western Values," said, "Pronouncements from the office of State Commissioner of Education Thomas Sobol are beginning to sound more and more as if they were written by Angela Davis." My credibility in the Legislature declined. The Board of Regents, to whom I reported, was supportive but bruised.

Dozens of letters poured in. First was the hate mail, which was so vitriolic and profane that I could not get myself to finish reading it. Hate mail was quickly followed by letters whose writers misunderstood what I was doing. Others understood, but pretended not to, and remained outraged. There were a few thoughtful critics. Thank the Lord for them. A few people wrote letters of support. Few journalists, if any, explained that the committee's report simply made suggestions and was not itself a curriculum. Having the word "curriculum" in the title was unfortunate.

The letters could be answered in private. Face-to-face confrontations with individuals and groups were more difficult to manage. How could I defend myself without being defensive? What could I say to friends who thought I had lost my mind? Where could I find a moment's peace when I was the subject of conversation in corridors, at cocktail parties, at dinner tables? I relied heavily on support from Harriet. Her courage was unwavering.

My lowest moment came as lunch hour approached one midweek day in Albany. I looked out the window and saw the daily lineup of lunch wagons across the street. Vendors were selling pizza, sausage, and other street food to state workers clustered at the curb. The park behind the Capitol building was buzzing as people came and went, sitting on benches, talking about the gossip of the day, talking about me. And I realized that I didn't have the nerve to go across the street to get lunch. I couldn't do it. Or I wouldn't do it. Either way, I didn't do it. There was no lunch for me that day.

For a long minute I thought I might go home. I realized that my car was in the alley beside the building and my key was in my pocket. All I had to do was get myself up, go outside, get in the car, and go home. But I didn't do that. Something stronger than public embarrassment wouldn't let me let go. I put the thought aside, and gradually immersed myself in the piece I had been writing.

CHAPTER I

Beginnings

The saltwater creek behind my grandmother's house was a magical place. The little house sat on a narrow road that led to the railroad crossing in Linden, Massachusetts. The creek ran under the road, about halfway down the slope from the house to the railroad. When the tide was out, there was almost no water, and I could walk from one side of the creek bed to the other on the big rocks that somebody had dropped there. When the tide was in, the creek filled deep enough to drown a small boy like me.

I remember my grandmother and my mother telling me about a boy a little older than me, who had drowned there a few years earlier, and how I was never to go there alone. But I couldn't resist. It was the most fascinating place in the world. I would hang over the railing on the bridge, look down into the creek, and wait for the tide to change. To this day I can remember standing precariously on the outside edge of the railing, peering beyond the marsh grass into the distance, striving to understand what was happening. I would throw small sticks into the water and wait until they were lifted by the incoming tide. They stopped, wavered for a long moment, and then were carried outward through the tall marsh grasses toward the sea, where they disappeared from view. The back-and-forth of the water made a powerful impact on me. I watched it happen right in front of me as if it were for me alone. Later on, grown-ups would explain about the moon and the tides, and I would try to get all that into my head. But all I really knew was that something very wonderful was happening, and I felt I was a part of it.

My grandmother lived in a small house built on a rock in Linden, which was a ten- or fifteen-minute train ride to Boston. The house was not far from the ocean. Frequently there would be a fresh east wind that was wonderfully bracing. It filled my lungs and smelled of the sea and adventure.

What I knew of life then was shaped by the women who lived there: my aunt March, my grandmother, and my mother. The household subsisted by virtue of March's job. The graduate of a "normal school," or teacher training school, she was unable to get a job teaching because of the Great Depression. Somehow, through friends, she found work as a secretary in the Middlesex County Commissioner's Office. The commissioners came and went in great profusion, but she stayed forty years and eventually ran the place. However, as a young unmarried woman starting out as a secretary in the early 1930s, she wasn't making a great deal of money. In those years, when people were out of work, there were no safety nets. There was no pension, no governmental support, no unemployment compensation. The churches helped a little, but the churches themselves were poor. What sustained us were my aunt's meager salary and the fruit and vegetables from the garden that my grandmother tended behind the house. She was a wonderfully abundant woman and a shaping force in my life. She picked wild blueberries and grapes; grew tomatoes, beans, and cucumbers for pickles; and canned grape and blueberry preserves in old mayonnaise jars. My mother helped her with baking cakes and pies and bread. Together they made noodles and homemade doughnuts, and brewed elderberry and dandelion wine.

Left to right: Tom's grandmother, Evelyn Naas Moran; Tom's grandparents, Evelyn and Walter Moran, and their children, March, Margaret, and Stirling.

Top: Tom's parents, Joe and Margaret Sobol, 1959. Bottom: Tom's grandmother's house in Linden, 1934.

I remember one cold winter morning at my grandmother's. I was in bed upstairs, tucked away beneath two feather quilts. There was no heat in the house except what came from the wood stove that dominated the kitchen. Around five-thirty in the morning, my grandmother went quietly downstairs to the frigid kitchen to start the fire in the stove. Soon the scent of wood burning and doughnuts frying drifted up the stairs as I lay snug under the quilts. Life for me in those early childhood years was sheltered. Though we were poor, it felt bountiful. I heard talk about money. I saw some of the distress, but I didn't know we were poor. We had plenty to eat, or so it seemed.

The family was what I had. The land in Linden was much less densely settled than it is now; there were few houses nearby and no young children. I was in the house with the women where life was stable and loving and simple. But there was fear that ran underneath, and it had to do with my father and my Uncle Stirl. Something was wrong out there in the world, something I wasn't old enough to understand. That world was where the men went during the day, and it was a troubled place. As suppertime approached, the women would worry about how the men would be when they got home. There was a threat of something external I wasn't privy to. Those thoughts made me uneasy from time to time.

After a long search, my father took the only job he could get: loading barrels on and off delivery trucks for Haffenreffer Brewery in Boston. He made enough money so that he and my mother could afford to rent a place of their own. We moved to a little street called Wyvern in the Hyde Park neighborhood of Boston. The house was a two-family duplex with two bedrooms: one for the parents, one for the kids. My brother Walter was born by that time. As it turned out, we didn't live there long, but it was the beginning of a whole new time. Life was no longer 34 Revere Street, where my grandmother, Aunt

March, and Uncle Stirl continued to live. We had moved to a different world, one of our own. It was exciting, but it led to a lot of bad things that came later on.

When my father went off to work at the brewery, I stayed home with my mother and my younger brother. It was a wonderful arrangement for me. I loved my mother intensely. We had an empathic bond. I responded to her moods and I daresay she to mine. I would follow her around the house while she did the daily chores: making the beds, doing the dishes, washing the clothes, and hanging the clothes outside to dry because, of course, there were no electric dryers. I had an imaginary friend named Mr. Bobbins with whom I would carry on long conversations. My mother must have thought it was odd, because she asked me to stop and to go do something else, but it never became a real issue.

The days passed in domestic tranquility. I was happy to be virtually alone with my mother. My brother was still a baby, and she was happy to be there at last in her own house with her children, awaiting the return of her husband from work in the evening. Many times I noticed how loving they seemed to be toward each other, and at those times I felt secure and warm in their company. Often, my mother and I would take walks while she pushed my baby brother in the stroller around the neighborhood, looking at houses. She liked the white houses with blue shutters. From time to time, when my father was with us, she would say, "Joe, someday I would like to have a house like that." On Sunday mornings, when my father was home from work, my parents stayed in bed, and later in the morning we'd have bacon and eggs rather than cereal or toast. Sunday afternoons we might take a walk out of our neighborhood, across the streetcar tracks and the railroad tracks into a public park and watch the amateur football games.

Without warning one day we moved to a dead-end street called Baker Place. I don't know why we moved. But it was there I had my first friends my own age, Joe and Paul Coughlin, who lived down the street. We played in fields full of daisies, clover, Queen Anne's lace, and some kind of yellow flower that blooms in August or early September. Butterflies, lightning bugs, and dragonflies filled the air. It was a beautiful summer. Then, suddenly, we moved again, to a modest flat on Dedham Road. We were living on Dedham Road when something bad happened. Somehow I had come by eight cents, a nickel and three pennies. I kept them squirreled away in the drawer of the bureau I shared with my brother. One day an organ grinder with a monkey came limping up the street. The man was lame, he had a wooden leg, but that didn't stop him from grinding his organ and making music. Of course all the kids ran out to hear him. I was enchanted by the organ grinder, the monkey, the music, and the excitement of it all. It occurred to me that I had some money. I ran into the house, found my eight cents, and brought it out to him. I thought that I was doing a good thing, because he had been entertaining. He had a bad leg and a hard life, and he could use some money. I felt pretty good about myself. But when the organ grinder left my mother was furious at me. She was almost never angry with me. I was a good little boy. I was the first-born. I did what I was supposed to do. But this time, she yelled at me, "How could you do that? Money is hard to come by. Don't you realize what we have to do to get eight cents? We could buy a can of tomato soup for a lunch for you and your brother for eight cents." I felt ashamed without knowing why. My mother's disapproval hurt and confused me.

We lived in two more places before we moved to Preston Road, a middle-class neighborhood in the West Roxbury section of Boston. We had a little flower garden in the backyard, and there were wonderful forsythias on the way to school. They were miraculous come April. I had never seen such a thing. I would have been very happy to stay at Preston Road forever. We lived on the first floor; on the second floor there was a German couple, who were our landlords. They spoke German most of the time. When war

Top: Tom and Aunt March, 1937. Bottom: 26 Cornauba Street, Roslindale.

broke out between Germany and Poland in 1939, they told my father, who was Polish, that we had to move. They weren't going to have the likes of us in their house any longer.

We moved to a place that wasn't anywhere near as nice. All these moves created an important pattern for me. This was a period in my childhood when our life, as pleasant and comfortable as it often was, also seemed precarious. The constant danger that we were going to run out of money wore on my parents and was subconsciously passed on to my brother and me. We learned that the rug could suddenly be pulled out from under us. People who had a grudge against my parents for reasons I couldn't possibly fathom could influence my life in such a way that I would have to leave my house and my garden, my friends and my schoolmates, and move someplace where it wasn't as nice. One day in early December 1939, when I was seven, my parents bought a house at 26 Cornauba Street in Roslindale, Massachusetts, another section of Boston. The sellers loaned my parents $200 for a down payment, which they repaid over the course of the next five years. The loan enabled my parents to get a mortgage from the bank. This was the house in which I grew up, and is the house I still dream about. I lived there through grade school, college, and my master's degree, until I was twenty-two years old and joined the army. Whatever else happened there, I developed a feeling of stability, of permanence and rootedness, that was vital to me because of the uncertainty I felt from constant moving.

There was a little branch of the Boston Public Library system up the hill from where we lived. My mother would often walk there with me and find books for me to read. One day she walked to the library with me and, because she was busy, told me to walk home by myself. It was a summer afternoon and there weren't many people in the library. I went to the children's corner and chose interesting-looking books from the shelf. The book

I was reading, about brownies and trolls, had so captivated me that when closing time came, I looked up and realized people were leaving. I stood up, gathered the books together, and began putting them back on the shelf. The elderly librarian with glasses and blue hair came over and asked me whether I wanted to take the books home. I said, "No, no." I shuffled my feet and looked down at the floor. "Thank you, thank you."

She looked down at the books in my arms. "Are you sure? I've been watching you read and I don't think you've finished all these books. Wouldn't you like to finish them at home?"

I said, "Well, I guess I would," keeping my eyes glued to the floor. "I would but our family doesn't have enough money for books," I whispered. She sat down next to me. "All you need is a library card. I will tell you when you have to bring them back." She picked up the book about fairies and trolls and said, "This looks interesting. When you return it, come to my desk and I'll help you find some other good ones."

When I didn't know what to say to that, she told me to wait and she would be right back. She returned in a few minutes with a library card and gave me two books to take home. I thought it was the most civilized, enlightened thing that had ever happened on God's earth.

These days, I often hear from people who believe anything governmental is inefficient and stupid and wrong and anything private is efficient and effective and right. When I was growing up, the government wasn't the enemy. The government was we, the people. The government did things for us, and we did things through the government that wouldn't have happened otherwise. What lifted my life and the lives of my brothers above the level of the streets and the little clump of woods behind our house were all publicly funded initiatives. Public schools. Public libraries. Public transportation. Public hospitals. The fields and playgrounds we played on. We the people had come together to provide these things for people who would not otherwise have had them. It was a miracle and a gift that has affected me to this day.

Left to right: Mike, Tom, and Walter, 1941.

When I was a boy, religion played little part in my home life. There was no talk of God, no talk of sin, no grace before meals, no bedtime prayers. Nevertheless my brothers and I spent much of our childhood and teenage years at the Church of Our Savior, the Episcopal church across Roslindale Square. Our first association with religion was a brief fling with the Congregational Church. My mother sent us to Sunday school there because we didn't have to cross a busy street. Our relationship with the church ended when we came home with dirty jokes we'd learned from the other children. Across the square from the Congregational Church was an Episcopal church, my mother's next choice. Because I was the oldest, I was in charge of getting my younger brothers, Walter and Mike, across the street safely. My mother was not involved with any religious community until much later in her life and my father, a lapsed Roman Catholic, never went to church. But my mother believed children needed religious education, so we went. I was twelve when I started attending Sunday school. By the time I was thirteen the church was an important part of my life. When I was not at school, sports, piano lessons, or my job as a newspaper boy, I was at the church. I attended services every morning and evening on Sundays, went to Sunday school and Young People's Fellowship meetings, as well as special events and trips, choir rehearsals, and Boy Scouts. Church fairs, picnics, and other youth activities filled my spare time. Actually, there was no spare time. My social life was based at the church. The Young People's Fellowship was a good place to meet girls, go on hayrides, and take trips to the beach. I had no sisters and attended an all-boys school. The fellowship provided a comfortable setting to interact with girls. On Sundays there were church services at which the choir, in which I was a soprano, sang hymns and anthems. After my voice changed, I sang bass.

In church, I grew up with the language of Thomas Cranmer's *Book of Common Prayer*. His cadence and poetry in English is stunning. How often

Tom playing the piano at 10 Claremont Road, 1976. Courtesy of Patricia Agre, photographer.

I have recited in church, "We have left undone those things which we ought to have done; and we have done those things which we ought not to have done."

If you read such prayers aloud, or hear them read aloud twice a week, year after year throughout your most formative years, the texts gain a resonance that becomes part of your linguistic DNA. The sacred music that accompanies the language is often Bach. His work is towering, intelligent, and beautiful. To this day, when I hear Bach, I say to my wife, "Can you imagine someone thinking of this? I wish I had written it." We had an old beat-up piano at home, and during my teenage years I took piano lessons from a graduate student at Boston University. When I was sixteen, the minister at the church asked me to play the hymns for the Sunday school service. I became acquainted with the organist, who taught me a little bit about how to play the organ. Another choir member who was an excellent musician also gave me lessons. A few years later, I became the choir director and organist. I played the organ for services, weddings, and funerals. It was a nice part-time job during college and graduate school, and for some years afterward. My brothers and I had great fun when I directed and they performed in Youth Fellowship productions of Gilbert and Sullivan plays. The words and music of those productions, which my brothers and I still reminisce about, gave birth years later to wonderful evenings with friends singing as they clustered around the piano while I played.

Making music has been one of the great joys of my life. Although I never became the musician I would have liked to be, I treasure the moments I had at the piano and the organ. In my late fifties, when I began to lose the use and feeling in my legs, I felt deep sadness at the thought of never playing the piano or the organ again.

During what must have been dreadful days lifting beer barrels for Haffenreffer Brewery, my father began drinking heavily. That's what the men who worked at the brewery did; beer was the one perk of their job. My father told us he wasn't happy and that he didn't like most of the men he worked with. As a consequence, he frequently came home drunk. My mother always had dinner ready for him, and he would sit at the table with my brothers and me and be sarcastic toward us, particularly toward me. I was skinny, I wasn't manly enough, and I read too many books. Typically, he would lean his elbows on the table while having his coffee with the canned evaporated milk that we used in those days. He would slump forward, causing the oilcloth on the table to roll up, then put his head down on his forearms and fall asleep. He worked every day of the week except Wednesday and Sunday. On Wednesday and Sunday, he would be pleasant, warm, and nice to my mother. He would fix things around the house. Monday, Tuesday, Thursday, Friday, and Saturday he would be drunk, mean, and arrogant. This upset my mother, which troubled me.

Years later I discovered that, during World War I when my father was an enlisted man, he received a wartime appointment to West Point, even though he never left the country. He was discharged after getting into a fight with an upperclassman. I also learned he had taken courses at the Minnesota School of Mining, and before the Depression had been married to a woman who, he said, was "too upwardly mobile." I wonder now whether those experiences and lost opportunities had contributed to the rage he felt when he returned home from the brewery, particularly toward me, his bookish son. Nevertheless my father, for all his drunkenness and anger, provided stability and a kind of rough authority in the house.

In all of this I tended to feel alone among my friends, though there were some I could talk to. The neighborhood boys were a rough bunch: cursing, swearing, and fighting were part of the their street ethos. That culture didn't work for me. The local boys made fun of me because my father worked in the brewery. They made fun of me because I was half Polish. They made fun of me because I wasn't Roman Catholic.

One night my mother and father had a terrible fight. I don't remember what they were saying to each other, but they were yelling at each other and I found it frightening. They went down to the cellar and I followed them. I was very scared. I didn't know what was going to happen.

I can remember the scene as if it were happening right now: my father, drunk and angry, is standing in front of the menacing furnace, a big coal-burning thing, with the door wide open. Inside I can see red hot flames. He has something in his hand that he is going to throw in. My mother is on her knees, on the cement floor, in front of him with her hands clasped, pleading, "Joe, don't, don't, Joe, Joe, please don't, don't, Joe."

I thought at the time, because of the war, my father had some kind of bomb in his hand. I ran upstairs. Though it was early, probably about seven o'clock, I didn't bother to get undressed but just took my shoes off and crawled under the covers, expecting something terrible to happen downstairs. I stayed that way, almost catatonic, the whole night. When I got up in the morning, my father was asleep. My mother was up and about. She seemed fine.

I didn't mention the fight, and she didn't mention it although she knew I had witnessed the entire event. I ate breakfast and went to school, but that night remains with me. Like my father, my mother was a complicated person. I had a daytime mother and a nighttime mother, and whatever happened at night was never discussed during the day and vice versa. My daytime mother was loving and dependable. My nighttime mother was often drunk and unreliable. As a result, I never felt comfortable bringing up what had happened that night or what happened other nights. I was always afraid it would happen again. Sometimes still, if there's a certain kind of midsummer day when it's very humid and hot in the afternoon and the sun begins to ease off a little bit, it just catches me the wrong way, and

I remember that scene by the furnace. Not much later, I became aware that a male friend of my mother's was spending a lot of time at our house. My father must have been working at the brewery when Daddy Jack came by. My mother instructed my brothers and me to call him Daddy Jack. I wasn't about to call this man Daddy Jack. I didn't like the guy.

One February day, my father was sitting teary-eyed at the little table in the kitchen. I was at the table with him. I don't know where my brothers were. My mother came in to kiss me. There was something odd about it, but I let her kiss me on the cheek. She went out the door, and I could see from the window that she got in the car with Daddy Jack and drove off. I asked my father, "Dad, when's Mom coming back?"

He looked out the kitchen window. "Don't you know?"

Puzzled, I said, "No, I don't know."

My father shook his head. "She isn't coming back."

That February day my mother, who had been everything to me, who was life and warmth and joy and everything that was life-affirming and good and secure, picked herself up and walked away from me.

The year my mother left us, my father was working a shift at the brewery that began at three in the afternoon and ended at eleven in the evening. He'd leave home about 1:15 p.m. in time to catch the streetcar and then the elevated train. Depending on how long he stopped for a drink with the men after work, he would get home at midnight or 1:00 a.m. or even later in the morning. We didn't see him very often.

It was school time, early February. I was twelve years old, my brothers eight and six. We had to go to school. My father was sleeping when we got up in the morning, and he was at work when we came home in the afternoon and at suppertime and bedtime. It was terribly important to me that we keep things together, that we make things right. What I was most afraid of was that they, whoever "they" were, would come and take us away and put us in a home someplace because we couldn't manage on our own. I was determined to manage the family. I kept the situation a secret. The neighbors all knew, of course, and they were good to us. Occasionally they would have us for dinner or bring us food to eat. Although they were friendly and kind, we were on our own most of the time.

I was careful never to tell anyone at school that my mother had left, and I told my younger brothers, Walter and Mike, not to tell anyone at their schools. On school mornings, I made sure my brothers were dressed and fed. Breakfast was simple, dry cereal, milk, and sugar, sometimes orange juice, but that was rare. Walter and Mike would walk to their school and I would take the streetcar to mine. At lunch they would come home and fend for themselves. It was up to me to do the shopping and the cooking, with my brothers working on the cleanup. I had never cooked before, so my repertoire was limited to hot dogs and beans, macaroni and cheese, pancakes, and other simple fare.

Tacked up to the mantel in the dining room was a chart I made that had our names and the daily chores everyone had to do. We all had to brush our teeth every morning and evening. We had to clean up our bedrooms. We rotated other chores, washing and drying the dishes, putting everything away, and vacuuming. It was order to the point of fanaticism. If the living room was out of order, I would spend lots of time vacuuming, getting each piece of furniture in the right place, and fixing the doilies on the chairs.

On the weekend I would make sure all the rooms were orderly so no one who might come to the house would think we couldn't care for ourselves, and take us away. I became the parent. My father, when we saw him, was always in a bad mood. We burned coal in the large furnace in the cellar, and sometimes the coal would run low before we could afford another delivery. When that happened, Walter, Mike, and I would walk with our wheelbarrow to the Roslindale Coal and Ice Company about three-quarters of a mile away and buy three or four 15-pound bags and wheel them home. Shortly after my mother left, I went with my father on his day off to get some coal. On the way to Roslindale Coal and Ice, he deliberately, or so I believed, walked out into the middle of traffic without looking and was nearly hit by a car, which screeched to a stop. I grabbed him by the arm crying, "Daddy, Daddy," and pulled him to the sidewalk.

Another night a couple of weeks afterward, my father took my brothers and me to the Wagon Wheel Restaurant, a sleazy neighborhood bar in Roslindale Square. I later learned that "Daddy Jack" hung out there, working sporadically. We were sitting at a little table drinking the nickel Coca-Colas my father bought for us, when my mother suddenly appeared. This was the first time I had seen her since she had left. She came over to our table. I stood up, moved away from her, and walked out of the place. After a few minutes, my father and brothers came out, too. Unsophisticated as I was, I knew my father had engineered the meeting with my mother at the restaurant. He knew she would be there. I knew that he had used us, but I didn't mind. I felt horrible for him because the pain he was feeling was so apparent. This went on for most of the rest of my seventh grade year, from February through March and the winter and into springtime and April. Then one day late in May my mother suddenly came home. I remember running away from her, outside. I guess I couldn't stand whatever it was that I was feeling. Johnny Maziarz, the kid across the street, asked, "Why are you crying?"

"My mother came home," I mumbled. He didn't say anything and I didn't say anything.

A few days later when I came down for breakfast, my mother, wearing her apron with large red flowers, turned around from the sink and looked straight at me. "Dad says you're still supposed to mind me." That bothered me, not because I didn't want to mind her, but because she felt the need to say it, that it needed to be said at all. Later that week, my father told me that my mother had told him she was home for good and would never leave again. My mother and father seemed happy together again. Once some

Top: Tom, 1949. Bottom: Tom riding his bike, 1950.

time had gone by, I enjoyed the most settled and happy family time of my youth. The sense of threat that had always been there seemed to disappear. Money was modest but better, and my mother and father weren't quarreling with one another. The threats and undertones disappeared, which stabilized the family. My brothers and I relaxed, experiencing a wonderful span of years, though always with a sense of wariness.

One day, at one of the church carnivals, I started to notice girls. How attractive they were! I had never felt that way before. It was maybe eight o'clock or a little after, and there was a beautiful sunset. I remember stopping down the street a few houses from ours and half-sitting on my bicycle seat, my feet on the ground, staring at that sunset for a long, long time, thinking it was the most beautiful thing that I had ever seen in my life. And I've never forgotten how I felt.

After that, such moments became associated with my feelings toward girls. I was longing for an ephemeral beauty that I had no words for at the time. Some yearning was coming from a place inside me that I hadn't been aware of before. I met Edie at Gloria's. Gloria was my piano teacher. She lived and gave her lessons in her parents' home down by the Charles Sumner School. Edie was a year younger than I and a year behind me in school, but she and I were about on a par in playing the piano. I thought that she was wonderful. She was beautiful. She was appealing in ways that I couldn't put into words. She played the piano. She read books. She was sensitive. I was George Gibb from *Our Town*. I was Penrod from *Penrod*. I was the stereotypical smitten adolescent.

I could not have been more in love than I was with Edie. I got up the courage and asked her to go to the movies with me. She had to talk to her mother about it, of course. Then I had to talk to her mother. They were an old-fashioned family, but that didn't bother me. In fact, that was part of the charm.

For our first date, we walked to the "Ori." The Ori was the Oriental Theatre in Mattapan, about a two-mile walk from where Edie lived in Roslindale. I thought it was the most beautiful theatre in the world. It had a Chinese-style décor, which I'm sure in retrospect must have been terribly hokey, but I thought it was wonderful at the time. White puffs of smoke that simulated clouds were blown across a deep blue ceiling and occasionally twinkling light bulbs blinked like stars. I thought this was a paradise. It was a paradise under any condition. To be there with Edie, watching *Gentlemen's Agreement* with Gregory Peck, was certainly heavenly. This was a full-fledged date.

There was a whole ritual in my mind that had to be observed upon such an important occasion, and it entailed not only the movie, but taking the young woman for ice cream afterward. In hindsight, I realize I was living *Our Town*. I asked her whether she wanted to go for ice cream. She said no, it would be better if we just walked home, she'd make cocoa when we got to her house. So we walked home. It was chilly by then. We were each wearing light jackets or coats. Suddenly, and really to my surprise, Edie put her arm around my waist and held on as we continued to walk down the sidewalk.

I've seen this and I've seen that, but if I could go back and feel Edie's arm around my waist the way I did when I was fifteen, I would. We went home, and we did have the cocoa with her mother. That's about it. I didn't kiss Edie until about a year later. One summer night when we were sitting on the stone stairs that led up to her front porch, I finally kissed her. Twice while I was still in high school, Edie and I performed at piano recitals given by Gloria's pupils. One year we played a duet, one of Liszt's Hungarian dances. The other time, she played her pieces and I played mine, mostly Chopin and Beethoven. When it came time to go to the senior prom I invited Edie, and we went. Her father drove us and took us home. I believed that I really loved her. I thought about her all the time. I looked forward to being with her, talking with her. It bothered my parents. My mother used to say to me, "Aren't you seeing an awful lot of this Edie person lately?" It became a standard question around the house.

My relationship took me away from the house and the neighborhood. It was part of moving out into a larger world. In the summertime, for maybe three different summers, we would go to the Esplanade concerts in the city of Boston, where the Boston Pops Orchestra, under the direction of Arthur Fiedler, would perform outdoors under the Hatch Memorial Shell by the Charles River. Even today, when I hear some of the Strauss waltzes or Souza marches, I think of the Esplanade, and of Edie. Sitting beside her on the streetcar, going home, after a silence I would say, "What are you thinking?" and she would tell me what she was thinking. Then she would say, "What are you thinking?" and I would tell her what I was thinking. It was adolescent, but I felt very close to her. It was nice.

One August I remember thinking that I had a wonderful year coming up. The fall was going to come. Fall, I would tell myself, would consist of football, apples, and Edie. I remember saying the phrase to myself again and again. The fall would be characterized by football, apples, and Edie, football, apples, and Edie. And it was. There were apples in abundance. They grew locally, and the ones we bought were crisp and tasty, as if they had just been picked. There was football. Even though I didn't make the Latin School team, I played on the neighborhood team, the Roslindale Panthers. We had games every Saturday or Sunday, and Edie was there. Edie and I learned some of the Chopin waltzes that fall. It was the year that Truman was reelected after the *Chicago Tribune* published their infamous "Dewey Defeats Truman" headline.

The following spring NATO was formed. McCarthyism was just beginning. Parnell Thomas's House Committee on Un-American Activities had just gotten underway. I began drifting away from Edie during my senior year in high school, even though I took her to the Latin School senior prom. By the time I went to college in the fall we were fast becoming distant friends. Drifting from her felt to me like a moral problem as well as an emotional phenomenon. If my relationship with Edie was partly what made everything right in my world, how could I justify leaving her? On the other hand, I thought, we weren't committed. We hadn't slept with each other. We had made no promises about the future. So, from a practical point of view, I owed her nothing, and we were both just kids. But in my head, in my heart, in my emotions, I felt that there was something clean and pure and right about my relationship with Edie, and when I was moving out of the relationship, I worried I was sullying something.

CHAPTER 2

Schooling

While on Baker Place I was enrolled at Sofia Ripley Elementary School, a little neighborhood school. On my first day of kindergarten my mother, misty-eyed at having to leave me, told me to remember to mind the teacher. That was the main thing: mind the teacher and do what she said. Before she left, my mother told me she would be waiting for me at noon when school let out.

I could read before I went to kindergarten. That didn't make me a boy genius. I was the oldest child in a family that read a lot. They showed me what letters were all about when I was very young, so it was just a natural happenstance of my home environment. I could count to one hundred and write all the letters of the alphabet. My teacher thought I was a phenomenon. I knew better, but I liked the attention.

When we moved to Cornauba Street I entered the third grade at Charles Sumner Elementary School in Roslindale. The classrooms in my new school and the other classrooms I sat in during my school days were not unlovely. They were large, with big windows, and the rooms were well-heated. The wood floors creaked a little. There were big wardrobes in the back of the room where kids hung their coats. Plants sat on the windowsills and books were lined up neatly on shelves. The desks were made of oak, with attached chairs, and were screwed to the floor. We sat in rows alphabetically. I usually had a seat near the window. I started sitting near the window when I was in the second grade and I continued to sit at the window until I was a senior at Latin School, where it afforded me a perfect view of the Simmons girls playing tennis in their gym suits. At Charles Sumner School, when the teachers said it was time to be quiet we folded our hands. We were polite to our teachers, almost all of them women and all of them, by fiat, unmarried. Their names all began with "Miss." From what I understand, a woman could not be married and be a teacher in the Boston Public Schools in the 1930s and the 1940s.

When I was older I used to wonder if it was really true that all my teachers were unmarried. Did some of them conceal the fact that they were married, or did they have marital relations outside of marriage? I didn't know enough to wonder whether they might be gay.

The Charles Sumner School was several blocks from my house on Cornauba Street and would be my school through the sixth grade. In the third grade, my teacher was Miss Phillips. In the fourth grade, I had Miss Clausmeier. In the fifth grade I had Miss Hartnett, and in the sixth grade I had Miss Lynch. They were of a certain age. They wore dresses with high necklines and cameos. Their hair tended toward the blue, and they were old-fashioned, strict, but I thought nice. Not all the kids liked them, but I liked them. I had to avoid being the teacher's pet.

The work we did wasn't terribly interesting. I don't remember anything I read. There were reading books, *Dick and Jane*, or something like that, but I don't remember because at the time I was reading everything in the Roslindale Public Library.

We learned addition in the second grade and we learned subtraction in the third grade, as if addition and subtraction had nothing to do with each other. We had multiplication that year too. We had short division in the fourth grade and long division in the fifth grade and in the sixth grade we reviewed everything. When I got to Latin School, we kept reviewing everything until we were in the ninth grade.

One week, in third grade, I was absent for a few days with the chicken pox. When I returned to school I discovered I had missed the three's multiplication table. I remember looking at the three's tables and realizing that it took no genius to understand the pattern. It was self-evident. I thought, that's how you do it. I looked at the four's, I looked at the five's, and it all worked out. I hadn't memorized the numbers yet, but I certainly saw the pattern. I could see the system. In short order, I showed the teacher how I knew all the times tables, and she professed admiration. My guess is my performance did not endear me to my classmates.

We also had art class. Once a week or every other week, the afternoon would be devoted to painting. I enjoyed painting. One spring day, those of us who could, brought daffodils to school. The ones I brought came from my father's garden. It turned out that there was a right and a wrong way to paint a daffodil. The teacher drew a daffodil on a large piece of paper and held the paper up for all of us to see.

"This is what a painted daffodil looks like and here's how you do it," she said. Thank you very much. One wouldn't want anyone stepping out of line. That seemed to be the teacher's attitude. The experience would have given Van Gogh a headache.

We had music, but not from our regular classroom teacher. Miss McGrath, the music teacher, came around once every three or four weeks to give us music lessons. Her hair was bluer than the other teachers' hair. She was the only teacher that I remember who wore a monocle. She liked to wave it about for effect when making a particular point. We would sing little songs using the solfège syllables: Do, Re, Mi, Fa, Sol, La, Ti, Do. That was music.

At recess the teacher would lead us into the yard, paved in asphalt, to play a ball game we called squash. Fortunately, I was good at it, so I could hold my own with the kids who were bigger and stronger.

We had report cards in elementary school. We received grades in reading, writing, and our other subjects. We were also given grades in conduct, effort, and penmanship. All during elementary school, I never received anything but A's, except in penmanship. I always received a C in penmanship and I hated getting the C because I was an A student. The truth is I had terrible handwriting. I don't blame the teacher for giving me a C, but what they gave you to write with in those days didn't help.

The desks had inkwells, holes in the oak desk in which you inserted a glass container, which contained ink that was mixed in the classroom. We had a sink in the room, where a teacher or some trustworthy student (never me) mixed ink powder and water, and then poured it into the glass containers in our inkwells. We wrote with black wooden pens that had tapered ends with grooves into which the point should be put. Into that groove, we placed a metal pen point, which we dipped into the ink. If we were careful and the pen absorbed enough ink, but not too much, we could transfer the pen to the paper without big blots appearing on the page. The problem I had was that when I put the pen into the inkwell, too much ink stayed on the pen, so that when I tried to write, the ink would spatter or drop all over the place. We were to blot the ink after we wrote. I used up my blotters more quickly than anyone else in the class.

The method we were taught to use when writing was the Palmer method. We were to hold the pen just so and skate on our little two fingers. We were taught to use our whole body. "Get your arm and shoulder into it," instructed the teacher. "Do your push-pulls and ovals." I could never do it the way we were supposed to. I would wait until the teacher walked to the other side of the room and her back was to me, whereupon I would take my hand and turn it on its side so that I could control the pen, using my fingers to make the push-pulls and ovals. Year in and year out the teachers gave me a C.

Most of my classmates went on to the local Washington Irving Junior High School. However, at that time, Boston had a number of special schools, such as the High School of Commerce, Mechanical Arts, English High School, and others. One of them was the Boston Public Latin School, the oldest public school in the United States. Founded in 1635, a year before Harvard College, it offered a classical curriculum including Latin, Greek, and other studies. Students from the city of Boston, if their grades were at a certain level, were accepted. I knew about the school from my aunt March. No one at the Charles Sumner School ever mentioned it. People in the neighborhood didn't know anything about it. My parents never told me about it. Aunt March, ever vigilant to learning opportunities, steered me to the renowned school.

For me, the Latin School was a sheltered place. The routine, the order, and the dedication to its mission all filled needs I had. I felt comfortable being there. It helped that I was good at doing what they asked me to do. It seemed the Boston Public Latin School was willing to take students that had C's in penmanship if they had A's in other subjects, so I was fortunate enough to be eligible.

Although I felt melancholy when the time came to leave the Charles Sumner School, I was delighted to be admitted to the Latin School and eager to attend. By the time I was in tenth grade my circle of friends had widened, and I had become involved with a group of students who remained together throughout my remaining years at Latin School. By the twelfth grade I thought pretty well of myself. I had a handful of friends. We'd play ball on the asphalt before school, and hang out throughout the day, have lunch together, and see each other in the afternoon before we went home.

As in most schools, there were the jocks and the brains. There were no thugs at the school but there must have been other groups as well. We were the brains. There were some wonderful kids. I wish I had kept in contact with them over the years. Stanley Cohen, who was the most brilliant person I've met in my life, wanted to be an athlete more than anything. One day we were playing touch football before school in the morning. Stanley was playing safety. When he knocked down a pass intended for someone on the opposite team, you would have thought he won an Olympic gold medal. I remember Leo Wolkow running to him, hugging him because he felt so good for Stanley. We were aware of how much Stanley wanted to have made that play. Everyone knew how intelligent Stanley was. We were in awe of him. Yet what really mattered to him was knocking down that pass, and when he did, we all rejoiced with him.

None of those friends came home with me, and only once did I go home with one of them. That was a special day for me. Myron Hamer, one of the boys in my group, invited a few of us to his house in West Roxbury. He lived across the street from the Roxbury Latin School and Myron said we could play tennis on the school's courts when everyone else had gone home. After tennis we went back to Myron's house. There was a baby grand piano in the living room. I sat down and started to fool around. "Play something," Myron asked me.

"Sure." I played a Schubert sonata. When I finished, Myron's family clapped. Even Mrs. Hamer came into the living room to clap. Then we had hot cocoa and I walked the three miles home. I'm not sure why that was the only time I ever went to a friend's house. I suppose it was because we lived in different parts of the city.

Every day after school, I took the elevated train and the streetcar back to Roslindale. It was a rough, Irish Catholic, working-class neighborhood. Where I lived, it was important to swear and fight. I learned to say "fuck" and that gave me some credibility. I had a few fights with neighborhood kids, although it wasn't a regular activity for me, which probably gave me some status. After the fights the other kids left me alone and I gained some respect. It didn't matter whether you won or lost. What was important was that you fought.

For me there were two worlds. One was the tough neighborhood at home, the other was the Latin School. I belonged at the Latin School and had little to do with the neighborhood kids. With the exception of sports, we didn't do anything together. But when they formed neighborhood teams, I was usually among the first to be chosen, and that more or less saved my life. At the Latin School there were kids who read, who were funny, who were interesting to talk to. They liked things other kids liked, such as baseball, movies, and (later on) sex. But they also had an awareness, a high level of intelligence, a keen sensitivity, and sensibility. They were different from the boys in my neighborhood. Most of the Latin School students were Jewish. I hadn't known any Jewish people before. There were no Jewish families in my neighborhood.

The teachers were called *masters*. The Latin School was an old-fashioned school. The building had an old part and a new part. In the old part of the school, the masters' desks were on raised platforms at the front of the room. In the new part, the desks were level with the students' desks. When a student stood to speak—that is, to recite—one began by saying, "Sir," and ended by saying, "Sir." The masters were all men, and they were wonderful characters.

Before it became coeducational, in 1972, the Latin School was boys-only, which was not an inconsequential matter to me. I had no sisters at home, only brothers. Having no girls at school and none at home made me uncomfortable, because it gave me very little experience when I became interested in them.

Instruction at the Latin School was formal. We studied English, history, science, mathematics, Latin, French, and German. Some studied Greek, though I didn't. Art was not part of the curriculum, nor was music. The masters would assign chapters in textbooks for us to read. We were to summarize the chapters and answer the questions at the end. When we were asked questions about the chapter, the questions usually tested our familiarity with the contents, not with what meaning you made of it, or what significance it had.

When we studied Latin, which we did for six years, we were never intent on what the writer was writing about. In retrospect, Ovid's

Metamorphoses could have been fascinating, but what we were told to look for were grammatical peculiarities. When we studied contemporary foreign languages, French and German in my case, we didn't speak it. To this day, with the assistance of a dictionary, I can make some meaning out of a French text and a little out of a German text, but I can't speak either at all except to say, "Chevrolet Coupe."

In my junior year we read *Hamlet*. I will always remember a quiz we had. One of the questions was "What is a wyvern?" The answer is a medieval dragon. The reason I was able to get the right answer was that "Wyvern" is the name of a street I lived on when I was younger. Nobody else knew the word or paid attention to it. I don't think that what the play *Hamlet* has to say about the human condition is captured by the answer to the question, "What is a wyvern?"

On the one hand one could argue that the masters were teaching us how to study. We learned how to get our work done in an organized fashion. We learned how to respond to demands that were made on us. We learned how to do a lot of work under the pressure of time and the competitive pressure to get good grades.

Speaking of the value of the academic program, I have to weigh the pros and cons. We acquired a certain discipline. We certainly got a thorough grounding in Latin and English grammar. Mario Russo, Phil Marson, and others taught us how to be economical with words, be organized, and make things coherent and unified. They were vicious with their red pens, but they really did teach us how to write, an achievement on their part.

On the other hand, we were not invited to think, ever. When we were reading literature, when we were studying history, science, or mathematics, we were not required to think. We were required to memorize the formulas and apply them to the given problems appropriately. Distance equals rate times time. I can do that in my sleep. There were aspects of the program that were outstanding, and there were areas that were deficient.

It wasn't all work. Because my name begins with an *S* and we were seated in alphabetical rows, I was seated next to the window. One spring morning I was daydreaming, staring out the window of my first floor classroom. The science lab was on the third floor. Seniors were working with rats. I thought I was dreaming when a mouse on a handkerchief with strings attached to the four corners came floating down the air like a parachute. I stood up and pointed to the mouse shouting, *"Ecce."*

I don't know when I discovered that I was going to college. It happened sometime when I was in Latin School, but it was never a decision. It came as a realization that going to college is what one does. My parents were supportive, but the motivation clearly came from the environment of the Latin School. All the students were planning to go to college. That's what they expected me to do, and that's what the teachers expected me to do, so that was what I planned to do.

In the summer of 1948, when I was sixteen and about to begin my senior year in high school, I had a new job working as an office boy in the Middlesex County Registry of Deeds. I put books away, paged people on the floor, and helped out when help was needed. The job required my taking an elevated train and two streetcars back and forth from downtown Boston each day. I remember that commute so well, those train trips, particularly coming home. Sometimes, when the heat was sweltering, I would suddenly get a sea breeze of east wind off the ocean.

In those days, the public Latin School enjoyed a special relationship with Harvard College whereby every year the college would accept a number of Latin School kids, most of us poor, to the freshman class. The students who couldn't afford to live on campus lived at home and commuted. When I graduated from the Latin School in 1949, there were 203 of us in the graduating class and seventy-seven of us went to Harvard.

I had entered the Latin School as a vulnerable, bruised boy, young for twelve, and immature. I came out of it much more sure of myself, with a more fully developed identity. I felt confident at seventeen as I left the

Latin School to enter Harvard College. By the spring of 1949, I had outgrown Roslindale, or felt that I had outgrown Roslindale, and was ready to leave it. I had outgrown the neighborhood and the kids I had known when I was young. I also had outgrown the church, or at least that particular church. I was drifting away from Edie. I had outgrown the Latin School. We had run out the string. Six years was enough, and I suppose knowing that it was the end made it seem all the more like an ending.

Because I was young, I thought that all that had passed was over, and whatever the future might be, it would be different. I was, of course, both right and wrong, because the future is always different from the past. I was right about that. But the past is never over. That's what I was too young to understand. The past remains with you and is part of you and continues to be part of you until your very last days.

The best thing about going to Harvard is having gone there. But you must take advantage of the situation. For example, as a Harvard graduate meeting with a stranger, you must establish your status as soon as possible. Obliquely introduced into the conversation, the fact provokes a variety of emotions in your respondent: surprise, envy, unease, hostility. It is guaranteed to give you the advantage in the contest that follows. Remember that generations of powerful men have exercised their intellect and their money to shape the nation and its culture. Draw upon them, and be at ease. You are among their number.

Note well, however, the importance of obliquity in the introduction. A true Harvard gentleman (or gentlewoman, though on that matter I am less well versed) never flaunts his superiority. He simply allows its aura to speak for itself. Thus when asked where he went to college, the Harvard man will never say, "Harvard." Rather, he will mumble, "Boston" or perhaps

"Cambridge," thus confirming the modesty of such eminence.

A more serious matter is the quality of a Harvard education. Any good analysis must consider its two chief components: the formal instructional program (courses, tests, papers), and the people and their culture (the interactions among students and faculty, the atmosphere of respect for *veritas*). One could be petty and note that the prevalent large-lecture method provides little opportunity for participation by students in class discussion or for a Socratic approach. I myself raised a question or made a point in class no more than three or four times in four years as an undergraduate. But Harvard's practice of assigning distinguished faculty to large undergraduate classes pays off. I concentrated on English and American literature, and the world and human nature were opened to my eyes by luminaries such as Perry Miller, Howard Mumford Jones, and Jere Whiting (Awak, quod he!). Enough said.

I cannot say the same for "the people and their culture," for I was a commuter. Every weekday morning I took the streetcars from Roslindale to Cambridge (about forty-five to fifty minutes). Throughout the morning I attended classes. At noon, in the building the college had designated for the purpose, I ate sandwiches my mother made for me and chatted with my Latin School commuting friends. By one o'clock I was back in the subway, on my way to my job at the newspaper delivery agency in Roslindale. At home in the evening, I read for my classes. On weekends, I pursued the same activities besides serving as organist and choirmaster at a local church having no direct relationship to Harvard.

The formal instructional program scores high. I found the work at the Latin School had been more than adequate preparation for academic studies at Harvard. However, I did not develop relationships with students like and unlike me, students who would become friends for a lifetime. I did not work my way upward through the ranks to a position of responsibility with *The Harvard Crimson*. I did not drop in casually to lectures, plays, and concerts offered in the afternoon or evening. I neither felt nor acted like a full-fledged member of a welcoming community. I felt more like a distant cousin who occasionally shows up carrying a peanut-butter-and-jelly sandwich when the guests are being served pâté de foie gras.

I am aware that one can take a different view of these matters. After all, the college admitted me and gave me financial aid. Otherwise, I would not have been able to attend. My Harvard education and degree have served me well. I am grateful for the financial aid I received. Although my contributions to the college have been modest, I have contributed whenever I could.

Perhaps I am more responsible for the quality of my experience than I would like to acknowledge. Inasmuch as I have imposed these limitations upon myself, I apologize.

I hope today's commuters feel more a part of the college than I did. Certainly, the college has an interest in the quality of life of all its students, including the commuters. Is there a dean for the commuter students? If so, does he or she meet with them now to inform them of ways they can participate in college life? If meetings were held when I was a student, I didn't know of them. Perhaps the culture of the college has changed in the past fifty years. If so, I am happy.

I'm sure Harvard's faculty is still as good as it gets. But its community may still need attention. If so, until attention is paid, both Harvard and the commuter students will be losing out.

In 1954-1955 I earned a Master of Arts in Teaching degree from the Harvard Graduate School of Education. It was a wonderful program and a wonderful year. About thirty of us students took courses in our field (mine was English) as well as courses in education history, philosophy, pedagogy, and a supervised internship in teaching at a nearby high school (mine was in Newton). The cadre was small and we worked long and hard enough that we came to know and learn from one another. Teaching and learning were at the core of all we did. By the time I left to join the army, I was determined that teaching and learning would be the core of my life.

CHAPTER 3

Korea

In April 1955, having completed the first eight months of my three-year army stint in training, I was on my way to Korea, on a flight from Boston to San Francisco, when I realized I was sitting next to the historian and writer Arthur Schlesinger Jr. He was reading an article in *The Atlantic Monthly*, but he must have noticed tears in my eyes. He said, "Are you headed overseas?"

I said, "Yes, I am."

He said, "Where are you going?"

I told him. He said, "Oh." He understood that in those years, Korea was not as desirable a post as Germany, for example.

After a pause, I said, "I took your course in American History last year." He said, "Oh," again in a solicitous manner. Then we were silent.

I reminded him of that episode decades later when I persuaded him to join a panel on multicultural education that I was convening. He served on the panel but he didn't recall the episode on the airplane.

It was hard to leave home. I had just married my first wife, Maria, and was leaving behind my parents, brothers, my aunt March, and all my friends. Maria was a part of the church crowd. She was eighteen and I twenty-two when we married. Neither of us had seen much of the world and we didn't have a chance to establish a home until I returned, three years later.

I arrived in Seoul in late April and stayed there for a few months. I was assigned to CIC, the Counter Intelligence Corps, at headquarters, on a little Army compound in a section of Seoul called Yung Dun Po. While in Seoul, I did a number of things. I typed new personnel forms for the Eighth Army. They had just gone from a blue form to a green one. The blue one, it said at the bottom of the form in carefully printed language, was obsolete but may be used. But we weren't using them anymore in our outfit. So we were retyping them on green.

I read files. I studied Korean, a little on my own and a little with some college-educated Koreans who gravitated toward those of us in Counter Intelligence because we were thought to be, intellectually, a cut above the average GIs. The Koreans would hang out with us to learn English, and we would try to learn Korean from them. It worked out nicely. We made some friends that way, drank beer together, that sort of thing.

What made my summer and reminded me of home was softball. I played softball for the Eighth Army—hard pitch, fast pitch, steal-the-bases softball—and I had the time of my life. It got me out of typing forms many afternoons, because the guys that played on the softball team were permitted to go to practice.

When we had games in the evening everybody would come out to watch. I played shortstop. During one game, at the crack of the bat, I pivoted, called off the third baseman and left fielder, and hurled myself along the left field line into a barbed wire fence. I still have some evidence of that day on my body, but the wounds were well worth the thrill of catching that ball.

My real assignment in Korea didn't come until September when, along with two or three other guys, I was dispatched to the CIC post in Inchon, a port city about twenty miles southwest, where General MacArthur had

Top: Tom, Korea, 1955. Bottom: Country road near Inchon, Korea, circa 1955.

made his surprise landing early in the Korean War. Inchon must have been a lovely place at one time. Rising from the harbor, the city sits on a steep terraced hill. The CIC compound, once the headquarters of the Japanese commander of the port in the era of the Japanese occupation, was set atop a hill with gardens of pines and azaleas checkering the hillside. The war had changed all that. Bomb craters were spread through the compound. The gardens had not been tended for several years. The remainder of my tour of duty was spent in Inchon, although I traveled around the countryside. The Japanese commander had lived in a large and extensive compound where we now stayed. Living in the Inchon compound were about twelve to fourteen Americans, all of us in the military in one way or another, and probably twice as many Koreans, interpreters, cooks, and housemaids who looked after us. We had the life of Riley if we wanted to live it that way. I didn't. I wanted to get away from the GI world and soak up as much as I could of the Korean world. Subliminally, I must have known that this would be my only opportunity to live in and learn from a culture different from my own. I traveled a lot in a jeep with my interpreter and driver, Min, a good guy. He was vital to my work because after my paltry few months' study I didn't have enough Korean to carry on a conversation. I knew enough to greet people in Korean, but I depended upon Min for substantive conversation.

When Min and I were in the countryside we drove by villages where there were clusters of houses. I witnessed people living close to the land, close to nature. Perhaps I romanticized what I saw but I believe there was harmony in the farmers' lives. When I look at some of the snapshots I took at that time, that feeling of their harmony with nature returns.

One day we visited a small village called Ansong. When we got out of the car, we stood and watched a man and a woman with their three children in a nearby rice field. They were cutting down the rice stalks, hitting them against the ground to loosen the rice, and bundling up the stalks to dry and use for their thatched roof. Their families had done the same thing for as many generations as they could remember. The growing and harvesting of rice was as much a part of their life as getting up in the morning and going to sleep at night.

Nevertheless, American culture had reached Ansong. One day when we were driving through a small village, I heard a familiar sound and wondered whether I was dreaming. It sounded like the ice-cream man who used to come to the Latin School at lunchtime. I turned toward the sound and saw a young Korean man driving a bicycle with a cart behind him. As soon as he saw Min and me, he started yelling, "Ice-a Cakee, Ice-a Cakee." I would talk about this for years.

The CIC had assigned me to participate in two studies. One had to do with refugees from the north and what they were doing, what their political alliances were, and whether they were arming themselves. You would think that the army could have found a better way to collect that information than sending somebody with a long nose, blue eyes, and blond hair out into the Korean back country. It was clear to me that I would only hear what people wanted to tell me. Nevertheless my willingness to be out in the countryside, to sleep on Korean hot floors, to eat Korean food, to talk politely and not act like a GI roughneck, got me access to people and conversations that I might not otherwise have had. My routine was to go out and talk to people who had been identified as possibly having information we wanted, and tell them I was in CIC. For some reason the CIC had cachet with the Koreans. The questions I would ask would arise from our conversation. There were particular subjects of interest to army headquarters concerning refugees from the north. Where had they come from? How did they get across the 38th parallel (the border between North and South Korea)? Why did they come here? Where were they staying? When I returned to Inchon a day or so later, I would write up my findings for headquarters.

I would never promise the Koreans I spoke to that I would do stuff that I couldn't do, but I would promise to carry their message back to headquarters, and try to make something good happen for them. I would get them to talk to me about the conditions under which they were living, what was happening to their families and so on, to see if there was anything that the American army might be persuaded to do, or even some quartermaster on the sly.

Occasionally someone on the base would give me a sack of oranges, which I would give out to kids in the villages. Those oranges were what I contributed most often. While I tried to get them what they needed, I never used political terms or military terms. It was always, "What was life like?" And the deal was that I never asked them to tell me anybody's name or anybody's identity. I simply wanted to know what life was like in their villages.

The American military leaders in Korea were afraid that the refugees coming down from the north would organize themselves into a Communist guerrilla army behind the lines. If I had picked up any of that, I would have reported it, but I never suspected anything. I don't know whether those situations existed or not, but then again, they would tell me only what they were going to tell me.

I focused on what was going on. What is the pattern of their life like? Who's calling the shots about how they are living? Where are they getting food? Are there schools for their children? Those were the questions I was interested in. Somebody whose name I never learned—a colonel, I think—up the line, sent a message down to say that this was good, and he wanted more of this kind of information. That made me feel terrific. Somebody appreciated what I was doing. But did I think that I was getting the whole truth? Absolutely not.

The other study assigned to me and one of my fellow CIC agents was potentially more intriguing. Prostitution was rife in Korea in those years, prostitution at all kinds of levels. The American military, the GIs, had money. They had power. They had freedom. And they had

Top: Inchon Harbor, Korea, 1955. Bottom: Korean children in Inchon, 1955.

testosterone in abundance, and they were going to take advantage of all those circumstances.

I learned later on that there was a hierarchy in the Korean prostitution industry. At the bottom were the first-come, first-serve women of the street, who might service several men an evening. Soldiers would go by the little hovels and see GI boots out on the stoop because Koreans don't wear shoes in the house.

Next up the hierarchy would be the houses of prostitution, which were better appointed, better kept, and usually run by a madam with a bed or at least a mat or a hot floor to sleep on. Continuing up the line were the dance hall girls. These were quasi-Geishas: entertainers, but in many cases also prostitutes. Sometimes it would be hard to tell the difference. Finally, at the top were the women who became serial mistresses of army officers, who would live with a guy for his tour of duty and then latch on to the next officer and so on.

There were sad stories of young girls who were sold into prostitution from rural areas where families had very little to eat and no other money coming in. Daughters in the family would turn thirteen or fourteen and the father would sell them into the city prostitution market.

We half-invented a dragon lady, but there was in reality a woman who presided over prostitution in Inchon, and who slept with the commander of the port in the American navy, a fact that we were able to document. We discovered that in all of this prostitution there was a lot of money changing hands. The United States Army wanted to know who was getting the money and what they were doing with it. My job was to find out how much money the prostitutes in the houses of prostitution were making and how much money the houses kept. I don't know what the Army did with this information. I was one young officer with one assignment.

What I do know is that so many petroleum products were available on the black market that some U.S. army personnel feared a South Korean army unit would get enough to fuel their tanks and jeeps. Many South Koreans were not happy with the U.S. troops. They saw their country being divided and they didn't like that. Although the South Koreans had weapons, they needed fuel. With black market fuel for their vehicles, a South Korean unit would be in a position to provoke conflict again and restart hostilities.

If you want to talk to prostitutes and to people who run prostitutes' lives, you do not pull out your wallet and offer them Korean money or even U.S. dollars. The real time to talk to them is during the day when they're not working. So that's what I did.

I talked to them and I got to know some of them well. I even became friendly with some. It was a complicated relationship. I got to know many girls and to talk to people who were part of that life. Young and healthy as I was, I never slept with any of them. I don't know why I didn't. I wondered about it then, and I've wondered about it in retrospect ever since. I don't know whether it was morality, because I was married, or whether it was timidity, because I was young and relatively inexperienced. I don't know whether I didn't because I was strong, or I didn't because I was immature. But for whatever reason, I didn't.

My wife, Maria, wrote to me that we were going to have a baby. Even after Sandy was born, it all seemed unreal when I spoke to her. Roslindale seemed worlds away.

The keeping of the armistice, in those years, was handled by teams of United Nations observers called the Neutral Nations Inspection Teams (the NNITS). They consisted of Czechs, Poles, Swiss, and Swedes. The GIs called the teams "CzechsPolesSwissSwedes," as if it were one word, like gesundheit. The army didn't like what the NNITS were doing and looked for ways to demonstrate their disapproval. For a period of months, there was a daily demonstration against the NNITS, against the CzechsPolesSwissSwedes, on the narrow causeway that connected Wolmi-do with the mainland. Army photographers would show up to take pictures of army trucks and people for *Stars and Stripes* and other newspapers. In order to get a good turnout, the Korean army would round up all the prostitutes from around town, and get them to line up. When the cameras were ready, the prostitutes would be directed to cheer and yell, "NNITS must go," or whatever they were saying in Korean. Everyone would have a fine time joking with each other. Then the cameras would stop. The photographer would put the cameras away, and the women would stop demonstrating and get back in the trucks. The next day, they'd be back again. That was the routine.

What I saw during my time in the Korean countryside was an ancient culture that had worked, that had an order to things, a harmony to things, a way of life and living. It nurtured its young people and respected its elderly. A young woman, went an ancient saying, could walk from one end of the kingdom to the other without being molested.

But all this had been destroyed, first by the long years of Japanese occupation, and then by the American military. Most of the guys that I was with thought we were doing wonderful things for the Korean people, saving them first from the Japanese and secondly from Communism. I have no doubt that we were saving them from the Japanese and from Communism. The problem is that in the process of saving them, we were destroying their culture. The Japanese occupation of Korea, from 1905–1945, was repressive and intentional. The American presence was more limited and unintentional. But both occupiers changed the way Koreans lived. And we certainly devastated a whole generation of women through prostitution.

Many of the most disaffected GIs were people we called Figmo. FIGMO was an acronym that meant "Fuck it, I've got my orders." As soldiers neared the end of their tours of duty, which in those years usually lasted sixteen months, they would receive transfer or discharge orders about two months prior to the end. The orders would tell soldiers the date they were leaving and where they would go next. Once a soldier got those orders, they felt no need to follow orders. If anybody of any rank asked you to do something you could say: "Fuck it, I got my orders."

So, people kept "Figmo" charts. We had big calendars and we would elaborately cross out, or sometimes embroider or draw pictures around each day, with little curlicues. Most people couldn't wait until the time came to go home. But when I left I was disconsolate, and I was not the only one. Some of us, including Peter MacFarland, Jim Harrison, and Bill McCloskey, had lived sufficiently long in a different culture that it was painful to leave it and go back home. Did we want to go home? Yes, of course. Would we have chosen, even then, to stay? I wouldn't have chosen to stay. I wanted to go home. But leaving still wasn't easy. It was a wrench. We had changed. There was something different about us, and I don't quite know what. For me, the feeling lasted several years.

The journey back across the Pacific took about two weeks. We flew over, but we came back by ship, on the USS General E. D. Patrick. We slept like sardines below deck and tried to get as much deck time in as we could. We watched a lot of flying fish. I remember spending most of those days with Peter MacFarland, on the deck, reminiscing about Korea. I do acknowledge that when we first saw American soil again, it was a cause for rejoicing. We had been at sea for what seemed an interminable period, almost two weeks.

It was a Sunday morning and we were all on deck. It was foggy. You couldn't see much in any direction. Suddenly, at one point, the clouds cleared, just enough to emit a shaft of sunlight. One of the guys in our group, Cornelius J. Kiley III, Harvard Law class of 1954, pointed to a building on shore that was now clearly discernible, and said in his most stentorian voice, "Gentlemen, there is land under the political jurisdiction of the United States." It was wonderfully corny of course, but everybody shouted, "Hoorah."

I took an airplane from Seattle back to Boston. God knows how many stops it made. I don't recall. But, during the last leg of the flight, I remember the pilot telling us that we were beginning our descent over Albany. When I was growing up, Albany was on the other side of the moon, and here we were beginning our descent at that point. We flew over what is now Logan Airport, went beyond it, and made a turn out at sea in order to come back into the wind differently. One of the first structures that I could see on the land was the white roller coaster at Revere Beach, which had always been for me a symbol of honky-tonk and reminded me of my early childhood years, going there with my aunt March and my mother and my grandmother.

It was as if this whole Korean world that I had been part of, with all its strangeness and difference and size and complexity, had shrunk down to be replaced by this little place of my childhood. It was a coming down in more than the literal sense.

CHAPTER 4

Teacher

Students ask me, "Why did you become a teacher?" I think they want to hear that I had some St. Paul-like epiphany on the road to Damascus. I confess to you that that was not the reason I became a teacher. The truth is that it was more gradual and plausible than that. From the moment I entered kindergarten I liked going to school because I did well there, and I felt comfortable. People in schools seemed to like me. I got along well. It all made sense to me.

Most of the valuable things I've learned in life were taught to me by one teacher or another: how to hold a spoon, how to manage the bathroom business, the fairness of taking turns, how to keep a bat level when you swing, how to turn your thumb under when playing a scale, the ecstasy of love, the responsibility that time attaches to it, the abiding strength of family, the central importance of work, finding the balance between forceful advocacy and tilting at windmills, the courage to be yourself, the greater courage to let yourself go on behalf of others. All these and other lessons I learned from teachers. Some of them were called teachers and some were not. Some were conscious of their teaching and some were not. But they were all teachers, and I am indebted to them all. Without them, I would be nothing.

I became a teacher for two reasons: I didn't know what else to do, and it looked like a good life. As a boy from a working-class neighborhood in Boston, I didn't have many models of people in business or other professions, so those lives looked remote to me. But I knew schools, because I began attending them when I was four years old and never really stopped. When I was a teenager I had a paper route in a section of the city much wealthier than mine, and I saw several beautiful houses owned by teachers who had kept their jobs throughout the Depression. We had moved around a lot when I was little, and that kind of stability was appealing. So I decided to become a teacher. My college classmates tactfully concealed their condescension.

When I graduated from college I was offered a full scholarship at the Harvard Graduate School of Education. In the absence of other models for professions or jobs of any kind, and certainly in the absence of any parental or familial counsel, I jumped at the suggestion of my church minister, the Reverend Eason Cross, and I accepted the scholarship. It was a natural evolution of what I had been doing. Reverend Cross mentioned how good I was with the church youngsters, what a good time they had when they were in the Gilbert and Sullivan plays I directed. I didn't know any lawyers, physicians, or stockbrokers. Judges, financial experts, and diplomats were simply not a part of my life. I'm sure people from all those professions were at Harvard, but as a commuter, I had little access to them. The person who knew me better than anyone was Reverend Cross. In the spring of 1954 I began practice teaching at Newton High School in Massachusetts and I fell in love. I loved the kids. I loved making things happen in that classroom. I loved working with the other teachers. People once again liked me and liked what I was doing. I had a love affair with the work. Perhaps I might have loved other work but I didn't know about any other work.

Years later, when I was a superintendent and then a commissioner, I became immersed in legal issues and lawsuits. I remember thinking about going to law school at night, but when the application asked me for my college transcript, I realized that too many years had gone by. My association with the law remained in my role as an educator and later as a policy maker. Before I left for Korea, Newton offered me a teaching position to begin after I returned. In those days it was easier for aspiring teachers to get jobs, but it was still uncommon for a school district to hire somebody three years out. Naturally, I was very happy that they wanted me so much. When I left the army I had a wife and a child and a job that I liked, waiting for me. I began teaching, and my life exploded. I embraced my students with a passion beyond my own understanding. They and the literature I was teaching were everything to me. I flew into that vast new space winged and exalted. I had never felt such strength, such energy, such fire, never experienced such engagement, such completeness. Some people discover that they have the gift of singing, dancing, acting, healing, or making money. I discovered that I had the gift of teaching. As I used it, I came alive, and it became who I am.

I don't know how long I could have sustained it. True teaching is intense, consuming, exhausting. I felt pressure to make more money, to control more of my surroundings, and to exercise broader influence. For decades I served as a school administrator and as a state commissioner of education. I worked with teachers, but the teaching I did was indirect, diffuse. When I announced that I was leaving Albany, Arthur Levine asked me to come to Teachers College. I am enormously grateful to him. He wanted me to work with school superintendents. I did, and I enjoyed it. But mostly I taught. I don't know whether Arthur cared about the quality of my teaching or not. It doesn't matter. At that stage of my life, I felt the wheel had come full circle and I was back where I belonged: engaging with students and exercising both my mind and theirs on matters of importance.

Although the lessons I learned about teaching in my early life remain true, others need to be added. While I was in the army, I picked up a book by Gilbert Highet called *The Art of Teaching*. Highet was an acclaimed professor of classic languages and literature at Oxford and at Columbia University. He advanced three principles of effective teaching: clarity, patience, and responsibility.

> The first is clarity. Whatever you are teaching, make it clear. Make it firm as stone and as bright as sunlight. Not to yourself. That is easy. Make it clear to the people you are teaching. That is difficult. The difficulty lies partly in subject matter, and partly in language. You must think, not what you know, but what they do not know; not what you find hard, but what they will find hard....And whenever possible, make sure you have been understood, by talking over what you have been trying to teach...
>
> The second is patience. Anything worth learning takes time to learn, and time to teach....Real teaching is not simply handing out packages of information. It culminates in a conversion, an actual change of the pupil's mind. An important change takes a long time to carry through, and should therefore be planned carefully and approached in slow stages with plenty of repetition disguised by variation.
>
> The third principle is responsibility. It is a serious thing to interfere with another man or woman's life. It is hard enough to guide one's own. Yet people are easily influenced for good or evil, particularly when they are young or when their teacher speaks with authority...[2]

These principles seemed right to me in the 1950s, and they seem right still. But I have long since come to think that good teaching is characterized by other principles as well. The list could become lengthy, but let me up Professor Highet's ante by offering four of my own.

First, good teaching cultivates style. It focuses upon general principles and the manner in which they are applied to concrete situations. As Highet said, "Real teaching is not simply handing out packages of information."

In his book, *The Aims of Education and Other Essays*, Albert North Whitehead also wrote about the use of information and the importance of style:

> Whatever be the detail with which you cram your student, the chance of his meeting in later life exactly that detail is almost infinitesimal; and if he does meet it, he will probably have forgotten what you taught him about it...Your learning is useless to you till you have lost your textbooks, burnt your lecture notes, and forgotten the minutiae which you learned by heart for the examination. What, in the way of detail, you continually require will stick in your memory as obvious facts like the sun and the moon; and what you casually require can be looked up in any work of reference. What is important is that the student internalize the general principles and develop a sense of style in their application...[3]

Second, good teaching is authentic. We are familiar with the pedagogic triangle: student, teacher, subject. Each relationship among these three must be real. The teacher must be genuinely engaged with both subject and student. The student must be genuinely engaged with both subject and teacher. The classroom is intense and personal. You can't successfully fake anything. Most especially you can't fake being what you're not. No teacher will ever be wise enough or clever enough or caring enough to meet the needs of all of his or her students, because those needs are insatiable and constantly changing. Most good teachers feel inadequate much of the time. But there is no use pretending to be what you are not, or professing to believe what you do not. Students will smell you out right away. The best you can do is be yourself, and hope that something of value is passed on.

Third, as Whitehead tells us, good teaching is religious. I use the term in its most liberal connotations. Transmitting human culture to another generation is a sacrament. Helping young people grow into the full power of their humanity is a sacred duty. To quote Whitehead one last time: "We can be content with no less than the old summary of educational ideal which has been current at any time from the dawn of our civilization. The essence of education is that it be religious."[4]

Finally, good teaching is an act of love. In its purest form, good teachers give themselves to students, expecting nothing in return. Nothing, that is, save the student's growth, on terms meaningful to the student.

I am not speaking of self-love, of the teacher as entertainer or master show-person. Such teaching has its place, but it rarely touches the soul. Nor am I speaking of seductive, selfish love, which uses the student to gratify the teacher's desires—a crossing of the line which, I can tell you from my years hearing discipline cases in Albany, is all too easy to do. I am speaking of the kind of generous love that enables teachers to sublimate their own drives in order to fuel the desires of others. This is the kind of self-deprecating love that allows teachers to shed their vanity and nurture students rather than assert themselves. This humble love leads teachers to strip their own knowledge and lay their own values open to the bone in the recognition that they may be wrong and their students right.

The gift must be given freely. There are rewards for the teacher, too, but they are not in extrinsic recognition or in some payback by the student. The rewards are in the doing itself, in engaging with students as they struggle to grow, in the very act of teaching.

Thus abideth these four: style, religion, authenticity, and love; but the greatest of these is love. I don't pretend to attain these ideals most of the time. But I cherished the time I spent with my students, and the ideals kept me reaching. And there is one final reward that I have not yet mentioned. As I march down the years on my crutches, the students keep me young. Do you remember what Robert Frost said about that? Let me remind you:

When I was young my teachers were the old.
I gave up fire for form till I was cold.

I suffered like a metal being cast.

I went to school to age to learn the past.

Now I am old my teachers are the young.

What can't be molded must be cracked or sprung.

I strain at lessons fit to start a suture.

I go to school to youth to learn the future.[5]

In August 1957, when I was discharged from the U.S. Army and appointed a teacher of English at Newton High School, Massachusetts, I was ready to begin my life's work.

Or so I thought. In actuality, I was confronted by a bewildering morass of questions that face most first-year teachers: What should I teach? How should I teach it? What do my students expect of me? What should I expect of them? What resources are available? How much work should I assign? How do I keep track of what we've done? How do I reach out to 115 students and help them make sense of our time together? When do we find time to do all that should be done? What do I do tomorrow? All teachers remember their first year of teaching. I don't know why we don't provide more guidance and support for teachers in their first two years, such as mentors.

Meanwhile, I plunged in, trusting that youthful energy would enable me to finish the year with my faculties reasonably intact. The experience was exhilarating but all-consuming. I worked day and night, relentlessly aware that I was flying by the seat of my pants, but confident of a safe landing because my students were taking the trip with me and would not let me fail.

Newton High School was and still is considered one of the best high schools in the nation. I had the privilege of working with the brightest and most eager students. We read *Hamlet, Macbeth, All the King's Men,* and *Portrait of the Artist as a Young Man.* Our discussions were lively.

One course in my program was different. It was a class of about twenty male students who had had difficulty with the school system. Some had disciplinary problems, some had attendance problems, some had been in reform schools. They were in what was called the Technical Studies Program. These students were notoriously difficult to manage. They were especially difficult with substitutes and young teachers.

In those years the custom was for suburban homeowners to display jack-o-lanterns on their stairs and porches, along with other displays for Halloween. Two or three weeks before the holiday, my own daughter had received a gigantic 110-pound pumpkin from her grandfather. We were very proud of it: we figured it was the biggest pumpkin in the neighborhood. But the day before Halloween it was smashed on the street in front of our house. My daughter was so upset she cried.

Before class the next day I was standing with one foot in the classroom and the other foot in the hall, so as best to monitor students' behavior before class. Then, for no particularly good reason, I heard myself telling the story to my tough students. What, I wanted to know, were the vandals trying to accomplish by such behavior? Was some teenager's thrill a fair trade for a four-year-old child's tears? On and on I went, on into class time, as I made one sententious remark after another. All I got back, of course, was sneers, which was all I deserved.

Late on Halloween night, when all the well-behaved trick-or-treaters had long since gone to bed, my wife, Maria, and I heard a giant rumble out front. I rushed out to see what was the matter. I opened the front door and there before my eyes were approximately thirty pumpkins, large and small, lit and unlit, all taken no doubt from my neighbors.

In class the next morning I saw nothing but grins from my charges. The young men displayed intelligence at least as impressive as that of my college-bound Shakespearian scholars.

Less than exhilarating was my salary: $4,600 for the 1957–1958 school year. By 1959, I had a wife and two children. Small annual increments notwithstanding, my salary couldn't support a family of four. I needed to find a second job. Luckily I had a skill to fall back on: I'd been playing music for local churches almost all my life. Throughout my fourteen years at Newton/Bedford/Great Neck I held positions as a church organist at Saint Luke's Episcopal Church in Allston, Massachusetts and Saint Stephen's Episcopal Church in Ridgefield, Connecticut. During summers from 1960–1966 I was a "Master Teacher" in the Master of Arts in Teaching program at the Harvard Graduate School of Education. With these second jobs, we managed to live in pleasant surroundings, but it wasn't easy. One consequence was that I didn't see much of my family, which wasn't good for my marriage.

Bedford, 1961 – 1969

My Bedford, New York years were seminal for me. A new superintendent was attempting to turn a quiet, satisfied, traditional school district into a noisy, cutting-edge place, and I was ready to be part of the action.

The superintendent was Dr. Charles O. Richter, a former assistant superintendent in Newton, where I had been working as a high school English teacher. "Charlie," as many of us came to call him, recruited me for a supervisory position in Bedford. The decision to leave Massachusetts and move to New York was difficult. I loved what I was doing and where I was doing it, but Charlie held four aces: an exciting new program, a kitchen cabinet of able recruits to work closely with the superintendent (including Neil Atkins, Chuck Fowler, and Randy Brown), the possibility of promotion, and more money. My annual salary in Newton was $6,500; my Bedford salary would be $11,650. I left Newton and went to Bedford. While working in Bedford, I took advantage of the GI Bill to earn my doctorate in education at Teachers College.

Charlie Richter was a human dynamo, bristling with energy and pithy remarks. The 5'9" Charlie repeatedly told the 6'3" Chuck Fowler, "Fowler, if I had your height I'd be president!"

My favorite Charlie Richter story concerns the board of education offices in downtown Mount Kisco. They were in the O'Brien building, a small, undistinguished, wooden structure on Main Street, with a steady stream of village traffic in front and no parking beside or behind it. The first floor was dedicated to O'Brien's Tavern. The second floor housed two rooms: a room in back which served as the office, and another in front for board of education meetings and for the superintendent. Local lore has it that during late board meetings, at 10:00 p.m., board member E. J. Van Allsburg would stomp his booted foot three times on the wooden floor beneath him and someone from O'Brien's would appear from below, carrying a tray of beers for everyone.

While I cannot vouchsafe the validity of local lore, I can guarantee the truth of my next story, because I lived it. Throughout his years in Bedford I served as a part-time speechwriter for Charlie, writing opening-day addresses to teachers, budget briefs to taxpayers, and holiday greetings. One December day I was sitting on a folding chair at a coffee table in Charlie's office, working on the annual Christmas message. Charlie was meeting with two out-of-town visitors, people he obviously wished to impress. He dwelled upon the beauty of the Bedford landscape: the granite outcroppings and the flowering dogwoods. He worked himself up into quite a lather. I was sitting off to the side, not part of the conversation, but I was listening. It was one of Charlie's best speeches ever.

When the visitors were gone, Charlie and I were alone. He said nothing. I said nothing. He walked over to a side window and stood there with his hands behind his back, staring at the scene outside: a jumble of cars and trucks, a filthy stream that oozed through overgrown weeds and rancid trash in the backyards of stores and businesses, an abandoned A&P

pushcart on one of several junk piles, which had been there for years. Without turning around, he said aloud, "Goddamn dirty town."

How can you not love a mentor such as that?

It was 1961. The baby boom was booming, and so was Bedford's enrollment. This small school district contained approximately four thousand pupils in four elementary schools and a junior/senior high school. All five schools were crowded, and all enrollment projections called for more, not fewer, students. The district would have to create more space. The best way to do it was to build a new middle school for pupils in grades 6 through 8. That would relieve enrollment pressure in each of the existing schools while creating an opportunity to develop a state-of-the-art school at the middle level.

I was not involved in making these sensible decisions. They were made before I came to the district, by Superintendent Richter and the board of education. But once there, I was delighted to participate in developing the education program. For the first four of my eight years in Bedford, I was a high school teacher and department head of English. For the second four years, I was director of instruction, a K–12 position responsible for the quality of the curriculum and instruction across all subjects and all grades. From these positions I took part in an effort to change middle schooling in America.

The full story is too lengthy for this memoir. I shall confine myself to two matters: some lessons learned about the process of creating a school and a few observations on the nature of middle schools. Both matters are drawn from my experience in Bedford in the 1960s, but are as true today as they were fifty years ago.

1. From beginning to end, the decision-making process was inclusive and transparent. Dozens of teachers participated, along with all of the district's administrators. Parents were involved through the board of education and PTA meetings, and through a parents' "curriculum council," which I chaired. Not everyone agreed with everything, but the buy-in helped the community see this as "our" project rather than "theirs." Including teachers and parents in the decision-making process was as helpful politically as it was pedagogically.

2. Also, from the beginning, we realized that the project would take many years to complete. The changes in teaching practice we were seeking could not be made by throwing a switch on a given day. Teachers needed time to live with them, to make them their own. We spent two to three years preparing the staff for the new school. We needed at least as many years for ongoing reflection and support after the school opened.

A Few Observations on the Nature of Middle Schools

Young people in early adolescence (typically ages eleven to thirteen years old) deserve an educational experience that is unique. A watered-down junior form of the traditional senior high school does not work. We wanted a middle school designed for pupils who are by nature curious, active, volatile, variable, and preoccupied with their peers. Most people at this age do not, by nature, sit quietly taking notes as the teacher lectures. They are more interested in themselves and their friends than in anyone else, real or imagined.

What would a good middle school for early adolescents look like? There is no single blueprint, but here is a short list of features characteristic of successful schools, all of which were present in Bedford's middle school to a greater or lesser degree:

- A "house" system, whereby pupils and teachers are assigned to "houses" or buildings in which they have most of their classes and special activities, remaining together for the full three years of the program. This form of organization makes it likely that each pupil will know and be known to each pupil and teacher in her or his group, thus ending any anonymity problems. The houses also provide a more gentle transition from the self-contained elementary classroom to the hurly-burly of the high school.
- Teachers who understand young people in early adolescence and who can balance academic demands with personal support.
- Teachers who enjoy working collaboratively with other teachers in teams and who know how to manage learning activities productively within two-hour chunks of time, as opposed to the high school's typical fixed schedules of five or six forty-five minute periods daily.
- Curriculum standards and student performance standards to inform instruction and assure accountability.
- Teachers who emphasize depth as well as breadth, inquiry as well as memory.
- Teaching that makes good and frequent use of group projects and hands-on instruction.

As you can see, the list is incomplete. I hope it suggests the kind of school we wanted to create, and says enough to support my assertion that the issues of fifty years ago are not unlike those today. We didn't revolutionize American middle school education but we conceived, built, and ran a damned good school—one that is flourishing to this day.

Maria and I enjoyed Bedford. We made many friends, enjoyed our house and our three children. Our neighborhood was full of kids. I worked hard, and continued my job playing a church organ in a nearby town. But my time at home was limited, and eventually my marriage began to suffer. Maria and I agreed to a separation. I left home for several months and lived in a small apartment but returned home to give the marriage one more chance. When I was hired to work in Great Neck, we kept the house in Bedford and I commuted. However, I had many evening meetings and was almost never home. The second and last year I was in Great Neck we moved to Huntington in the hopes that the family could be together. The move turned out to be poor for everyone. Both Maria and the kids missed their Bedford life and I was still rarely home. By 1971 we had gotten a divorce.

When I assumed the position of director of secondary instruction in Great Neck, New York, in September of 1969, I began by dealing with matters that are standard fare for anyone in such a position: personnel, negotiations, curriculum, and the testing program. Before long, however, I realized that what made the job unique was the war in Vietnam and its social fallout on our students.

By 1968 we had committed hundreds of thousands of American troops to Vietnam, there had been tens of thousands of American casualties, and God only knows how many Vietnamese casualties on both sides. The war played out on television in a way that no war ever had, with nightly depictions of bombings, napalming, and body bags arriving home in helicopters. To say the country was divided is an understatement. The country was torn in two. Either you supported the war or you opposed the war. It was virtually impossible in those years, at least as I experienced them, to be neutral. The war pitched husband against wife, brother against brother, young against old. Neighbors in support of the war stopped talking to their neighbors who opposed it. Dinner parties that started with quiet conversation were ruined by loud arguments and ended with angry guests stomping out. Rallies, demonstrations, and marches were an everyday occurrence.

I personally thought the war was wrong. That's not to say that what I believed made me righteous or better than anyone. That's simply what I felt, and I felt it strongly. One of the things that made me feel the war was wrong was the experience I had in Korea. We had resisted the encroachment of the North Koreans and the Chinese, and in the process of doing so, we had inadvertently trampled upon an ancient culture. Now, only a few years later, it felt like we were wiping out another culture and I couldn't see any justification for doing so. Some of my friends agreed with me. Some did not. We avoided discussion about the war for the sake of our friendship, but it wasn't easy.

While the war in Vietnam was being waged, a cultural revolution was sweeping the nation at home. It's hard to describe it to anyone who didn't live through it. A sea change in attitudes toward established authority, established convention, and established ways of thinking about the world grew out of the universities and colleges, spreading throughout the nation like an uncontainable epidemic. Reasoned order, self-control, and respect for authority were no longer dominant virtues among young adults. Sex, emotion, intuition, imagination, and passion were prized. There was an assault on convention of every kind in art, music, dress, and manners. The cultural upheaval that occurred in the 1960s was profound and dramatic and it affected all parts of life, including the schools.

Everywhere throughout the society, but even more so in the suburbs close to New York City, young people were challenging adult authority over everything, from stupid little things like not chewing gum in school to the legitimacy of the national government to carry on the war, or to govern at all for that matter.

It came as no surprise that some Great Neck high school students wanted to be represented on the board of education. Many adults said students had no business being on the board, that they weren't mature enough for that role. In order to appease them both, we established positions called "student delegates" to the board of education. The student delegates could attend all of the public meetings and some, if not all, of the closed meetings of the board, and would be given time on the agenda to speak to their and the board's issues. The arrangement worked well, and the parties learned from each other.

At the request of many of the junior and senior young men, the student delegates suggested the high school provide draft counseling. The board agreed and asked me to arrange for it. It was something students wanted but it was politically controversial. The program I set up spoke to many concerns. It described the laws and what student obligations were, as well as what their choices were. It looked at what procedures needed to be followed, who draftees might talk to, and what to do about appeals. The program didn't advocate, but it provided reliable information to concerned young men. In order to keep it from being publicly funded, we engaged a non-profit group to run the program, but there were many Great Neck people who didn't want us to do even that.

In 1969 I was thirty-seven years old: old enough to be very much of the establishment. On the other hand, I was young enough and sympathetic enough to connect with the people who were leading the rebellion. The role that I undertook in Great Neck was to be the school person who would try to bridge the widening gap between student rebels and established school officials. I worked closely with student protest leaders both in and out of school. I spent time hanging around the places where students tended to congregate, including ball fields and the cafeteria.

In the spring of 1970, students were demonstrating against the war on the campus of Kent State University. The Ohio State National Guard was summoned to restore order, and in a tragic turn of events shot thirteen students, killing four and wounding nine others. Newspapers and television journalists covered the story, and photographs of the event were published everywhere. America was in a rage. At almost the same time, President Nixon announced a campaign to bomb Cambodia, which had been previously regarded as neutral. Nixon claimed the North Vietnamese were using parts of Cambodia to store material and men, which was probably true, but it represented a very unwelcome escalation of hostilities. Students in Great Neck as well as across the country reacted with fury to both the shootings at Kent State and the invasion of Cambodia. The morning after the news was announced, the students poured out of the South Senior High School to rally around the flagpole. They had every intention of bringing the flag down, at least to half-mast.

A group of students who supported the war commanded the high ground, literally, and surrounded the flagpole first. No way were they going to see the American flag dishonored. One of the students, worried about a possible fight, called my office in the central administration building to tell me what was happening. When I got there I saw a group of thirty to forty boys guarding the flagpole. Hundreds of students who wanted to take the flag down surrounded them, chanting, "Take it down, take it down." We were about to have a melee.

John L. Miller, who had been superintendent in Great Neck for twenty-six years, and who was set to retire in a few months, was giving orders to the staff to suspend anybody who left a classroom. An aging patrician dressed in a three-piece blue suit and a gold chain strung across his vest with a Phi Beta Kappa key hanging from it, he looked as if he came from another century. Student uprisings were not his thing. He stood in the middle of two thousand students, all of them milling about and shouting profane slogans, ready to shed blood over this flag. Suspending them would have looked good on paper, but it clearly wasn't going to change what was happening.

Thankfully, Mort Abramowitz was there. Mort was the assistant superintendent, a man about fifteen years older than me, and a good friend who became the superintendent when I became the assistant superintendent the following year. He was terrific. He suggested we talk it out, and that I be the one to communicate with the students. Instead of having a free-for-all, we asked everybody to go back into the building and we would vote on what to do with the flag. It was that simple.

This was my addition to the plan: whoever lost the vote would still have some minority rights, so we would reserve some time for them. If the vote was to take the flag down (as we all believed it would be) there would have to be some time left when the flag would go back up since other students who were part of the community clearly wanted it.

It took a lot of talking with the students to get them to feel that they weren't being conned or co-opted. They finally bought into it and went back into the school building. There was no fight. They took the vote. The vote was to take the flag down, of course. It remained down all afternoon. At 4:00 p.m. it was raised back up, as we had agreed, and it stayed there until closing hour, about 6:00 p.m.

Students from the two high schools, South and North, and some of the middle schools were planning a huge demonstration for the next day. Along with all of the secondary-level students from the adjoining towns of Manhasset and Roslyn, the Great Neck students were going to walk out of school at 10:00 a.m., march through town, and assemble on a big field in Manhasset. Once we learned about the students' plan, the question was what to do.

John L. Miller suggested posting teachers at the door and not allowing anybody out. The other two possibilities were to stick to our jobs and conduct classes with those who were left, or walk with them. We had a fevered debate about what to do. Of course, there wasn't any right thing or wrong thing. I remember making the point that these were extraordinary times and required extraordinary measures. Board members entered the debate. One member said, "You can't walk out, that's abdicating your authority to the students. It's inviting anarchy. We can't have that."

I knew what I had to do. I had established my bona fides with those students. They trusted me. They connected with me. I had been standing up for them. They had gone along with me when we tried to coax them back into the building the day before. I said, "Mort, you stay here. You're too important to do this. You stay here, but I'm going to walk with the students tomorrow morning."

At 10:00 a.m. the next morning we walked out of the South Senior High School, went over to Middle Neck Road, joined the students from North High School, and marched together down to the field in Manhasset. There must have been six or seven thousand high school students on a huge, sprawling piece of land. They had a planned program with several speakers. It was important for me to talk with them, but not to speak. Most of the speakers were students. They were terrific! The entire march and program was peaceful. They were out of school for about two hours, after which they returned to school and finished the school day. The teachers let them back in. Different teachers treated their students differently, of course, but most classrooms settled right down and resumed academic work.

When the speeches were finished, I hung around the field for a while to make sure all the students had gone back to school. When I was leaving the field, I looked back on the field that had just held thousands of juiced-up adolescents and saw that there were no lingerers, no scraps of paper, not the slightest sign of any disturbance. I remember being so proud of them!

Over the years, occasionally I have met a student who was involved in this event. None of us who were there will forget the day that we marched down Middle Neck Road to protest the bombing in Cambodia. I don't know if what we did was right or wrong. You could argue that until dooms-day. But it felt right for me and for those students at that time.

The confrontation at the flagpole and the march on Manhasset were stu-dent-initiated events, but teachers and school officials also worked to make the education program more responsive to the mood and temper of the times. Our most significant initiative was the creation of an alternative school.

Throughout the spring and summer of 1970, I worked with a dedicated core group of students, teachers, and parents to develop a plan for an alterna-tive high school. The school would enroll a few hundred students who volun-teered to participate and whose parents approved. It would be small enough to create a supportive interpersonal environment for students and teachers, would hold students responsible for their own learning, and let students set their own standards for personal behavior. We found a place for such a school in an abandoned church and rectory building in the downtown village of Great Neck. We called it the Village School.

Many of the features we began in the Village School have become stan-dard in school reform projects elsewhere. We limited the size of the school to 150 students. Students would participate in school governance, but not through the archaic arrangements that had previously existed. Students and teachers would exercise authentic ownership. They would make the rules they then had to live by. They created committees to enforce the rules. They held weekly community meetings to hash out current issues.

When the school first opened, much time was devoted to less philosophi-cally pertinent issues, such as: where should we put the Coke machine? Who should be allowed to play on the Ping-Pong table? What if somebody else is studying or not?

But we also had interesting discussions about what constitutes a sound lib-eral education, how to decide what should be studied, and who had the right to make those decisions. People argued all that out at the community meetings.

We also established core groups in which each teacher was responsi-ble for the education of between six and eight students, regardless of the teacher's subject matter background. The core groups met once or twice a week to review students' progress and make plans for the coming week. I got the idea for core groups from the teachers I taught at the Harvard Graduate School of Education in the summer. I knew the idea worked well there, so I expected it to work well here.

There was a lot of individual instruction and small group instruction. In addition to conventionally certified teachers, we enlisted people from the community who were knowledgeable in specific areas to pass on their skills and experience.

We required a portfolio of achievement at the end of the year from each student. It wasn't enough to pass a test. Sudents had to exhibit material they had written explaining their work, or perform a demonstration of what they had learned. The portfolio was judged by a jury of people qualified to review it, not only the student's regular teachers but by professionals from the community. Because we felt we were close enough to every student so that each should succeed, when a student didn't pass muster we took it as a great failure on our part. The dropout rate was less than three percent. Before we started the school, we talked to college admissions officers about submitting students' portfolios as part of the admission process, and they encouraged us to go ahead.

I do not claim that I invented the school from my own brow. The credit is due to the teachers and students who worked so long and hard to bring it into existence and to sustain it for so many years. But I am proud of my share in the achievement. We created the Village School in 1970. And you know what? It's still here. Over forty years later, it is flourishing. We must have done something right!

CHAPTER 5

Scarsdale

S ome parents in Scarsdale had heard about the Bedford middle school and my role in its creation. They recommended me to Carroll Johnson, who was running the search for Scarsdale's superintendent and was a member of the faculty at Teachers College. Carroll had been a superintendent of the school system in White Plains and is still respected by superintendents all over the nation. I was interviewed and eventually hired by the Scarsdale board.

Although my marriage with Maria was foundering, we decided to move back to Westchester. We sold our house in Huntington and bought a house in Scarsdale. At that time, the board expected their superintendents to live in town. Living in Scarsdale, Maria would be close to Bedford where she had many friends. Things did not improve between us. By March we were separated. I moved to a small apartment in White Plains. Each of us consulted lawyers. After several months of negotiations, Maria and I agreed to the terms of our legal separation, which became the terms of our divorce.

Our children completed the year in the Scarsdale schools. By the summer of 1972, Maria had sold the house in Scarsdale and moved back to

Bedford with our children, Sandy, Tommy, and Michael. Sandy was off to Hampshire College for her freshman year. It was not a happy time for anyone in the family, but it had been coming for a long time.

I was appointed the superintendent of schools in Scarsdale, New York in the summer of 1971. I was thirty-nine years old. One of my first conversations was with an able and determined young high school teacher named Judy Codding. As I was getting out of my car in the high school parking lot one morning, I was surrounded by a small group of teachers. Speaking on their behalf, Ms. Codding asked me, "Can we have an alternative school?"

I looked around, and seeing no students, replied, "Where are the kids?"

She looked back and smiled, "I'll find them!"

I knew then we were going to have a second alternative school.

Judy knew that the Village School in Great Neck had been conceived by a small group of students with adult help. She understood that student ownership would be of essence to creating a new school, and that student ownership required student leadership. Within days we formed a committee of students, teachers, and parents to conceive of a Scarsdale Alternative School, planning to open one year later, in September 1972. The school opened on time and is in operation still, some forty years later.

The Village School in Great Neck and the Alternative School in Scarsdale are similar in all important respects. They serve similar populations, share a common purpose, and practice a kind of education frequently called "progressive." Both schools give students more freedom and impose more responsibility. Both schools are organized into core groups and hold weekly community meetings. Both schools have low dropout rates and high college placement rates. But the Alternative School is not a copy of the Village School. Rather, each has learned from the other while preserving their own uniqueness. For example: the Alternative School made efforts to transform Lawrence Kohlberg's ideas for a "just community" from an abstract idea into a living reality, something that had not interested the Village School. I taught a course for the Scarsdale Teachers Institute called

The Hidden Curriculum, which included among the readings for the class, the work of Larry Kohlberg, a psychologist and philosopher.

Kohlberg built his theory of moral development on work by Jean Piaget. Piaget had discovered that children younger than ten or eleven believe rules are sacred, that they can't be changed. Children older than ten or eleven understand that rules can be altered if everyone involved agrees, and that rules exist so that people can live together in a community. Younger children measure the severity of acts that break the rules by the damage they do, but older children can judge the intentions of the rule-breaker. If one child, while helping his mother, breaks six cookies and another child breaks one cookie that he has stolen, children younger than eleven will likely say the child who broke six cookies is more at fault than the child who broke one. Older children can account for the intentions of the first child and say that the child who broke one stolen cookie should be more severely punished.

Kohlberg took Piaget's theories several steps farther. He interviewed seventy-two boys, ten and older, from middle and low class families. Later, he interviewed younger boys. Based on these interviews, he developed six stages of moral development, using Piaget's stages as his first two.

The founding teachers of the Alternative School (Judy Codding, Tony Arenella, and Dawes Potter) and a committee of students wanted to implement a just community, as mentioned in Kohlberg's work. They had heard about a school in Boston, associated with Kohlberg, which was a just community. I approved the idea and worked with them.

A just community is small so that individuals who form the group matter to each other. Students take a course in ethical reasoning. With the guidance of a teacher, they learn about Kohlberg's stages of morality.[6] The just community is a democratic community that operates in a just way where the emphasis is placed on caring and concern for others, conflict resolution skills, and academic commitment.

The center of the just community is the weekly community meeting when students and teachers discuss issues that affect community life. Anyone in the community may raise an issue. For example, should students help another student with a problem when help is requested? Is it acceptable for members of the community to be verbally abusive to each other? Should drugs and alcohol be allowed on the school's property? What sort of consequences should the fairness committee deliver if people break rules made by the community? And so forth.

Students and teachers have an equal voice in these matters. The teacher, however, might bring up Kohlberg's stages of moral development, urging students to reach for the next step in reasoning. Fairness and justice for all members of the community is a goal. Rather than reaching decisions by a majority vote, the group works toward a consensus. One might argue, as many did, why a 'just community.' Why not just have a small community school? The answer lies in Lawrence Kohlberg's "Moral Education: A Response to Thomas Sobol" in *Educational Leadership*: "[W]e compared change in the Scarsdale alternative school, with its "just community" governance process, with change in a Mamaroneck alternative school without democratic self-governance. There was significantly more growth on both the Harvard stage measure and the D. I. T. (Defining Issues Test) in the Scarsdale alternative school than in the Mamaroneck school."[7]

My office was in a wing of the high school building. In good weather, students would congregate in the driveway, making it difficult for cars to get to the parking lot. One day it was particularly crowded. Rather than move, students surrounded my car. One female student climbed on the hood of my car yelling expletives. I asked the young woman her name. She asked me who I was. I answered, "I'm the Superintendent of Schools." She took her time getting off the car, and with the crowd of students, shuffled out of the way. Shortly afterwards, I received a call from Tony Arenella. Another student had reported the incident to him. It turned out that the young woman who had stood on the hood of my car was an A-School student (the term for a student of the Alternative School). Tony wanted me to appear at a fairness committee meeting and relate what had happened. "Tony, I really don't want to make a big thing of this. Why don't I ask her mother to come in with her and we'll talk about it in my office?"

"Tom, please. It's a teachable moment."

With some misgivings, I went, and along with the small group of teachers and students, sat on the floor of the old building in which the school was housed. I reported what had happened. The student was silent. She shrank into her chair. The committee was horrified. They were used to infractions like cutting classes and alcohol and drug use, but nothing as colorful as this. They also knew that, bottom line, I was responsible for the school's existence. I don't remember all the committee decided she should do. However, I do recall she was required to write an apology to me, which she did. Tony was correct. It was indeed a teachable moment and an unforgettable one.

It's hard to know how many other schools the Great Neck Village School and the Scarsdale Alternative School have influenced. There is a seminal quality about them. They were charter schools before there were charter schools.

I met Harriet through the schools. The first time I remember meeting her was at a PTA meeting. I noticed her and remembered that she had long hair and wore sandals. She was intelligent and attractive.

Harriet was the new PTA president of Heathcote Elementary School and later was involved in getting the Alternative School going. Before having children, she had been a teacher and she had been a substitute in the Scarsdale schools since she had moved there in 1965. After we were married, she stopped her involvement in Scarsdale for my sake, began to write children's books and taught creative writing in the White Plains Adult School, and later in the Scarsdale Adult School, which is independent of the public school system. For the past twelve years, she has also run several book groups. Her oldest child, Greg, is severely retarded. He has lived in group homes since he was nine. When I met Harriet, her son Jeff and

Harriet, 1979.

her daughter Jenny were in the early grades of elementary school. Her ex-husband lived nearby. When Jenny and Jeff were young, their father was at our house almost every day after work, visiting his children. My children were always welcome for holidays and whenever they wanted to drop by.

It would be dishonest to say that everything went smoothly all the time. I felt guilty about living with Harriet's children rather than my own, particularly Michael, my youngest. As might be expected, Harriet was protective of her children, although she was terrific with mine. I tried to see my kids as much as I could but it wasn't the same as living in the same house with them.

I worked long hard hours and was out many nights. By the time I got home, I wasn't up for much conversation, which was a problem for Harriet. When I was able to get home for dinner, my mind was on the meeting I had to attend after we ate. I could be impatient and difficult.

Money was a problem. I had given the house in Scarsdale to Maria. The summer after our divorce, she sold it and used the money to buy a house in Bedford. It was important to me that my kids have a nice place to live. My agreement with Maria when we were divorced spelled out alimony and child support, which I religiously paid. I was responsible for college tuition. Sandy began college the year after our divorce and Tommy a few years later. It was a hard time but I loved Harriet and I liked my job. Whenever I had free time in the afternoon, I painted the house, wallpapered, or worked in the garden. Within three years of our marriage, Harriet and I each lost one of our parents, Harriet her mother, and I, my father.

Nevertheless, most of the time I was happy, and particularly happy to be married to Harriet. We had been married five years when I wrote the following lines for publication in the *Twenty-Fifth Anniversary Report* of Harvard's class of 1953:

I am the Superintendent of Schools in Scarsdale, New York. I work hard, gladly. The job fits me. Critics and the unions notwithstanding, to pursue the best in public education seems as important now as when, fresh from Latin School, we ate lunch each day at Dudley House, and I thought it was named for the subway station.

I live in a strong, full house. Inside are my second wife, Harriet, and her children, Jennifer and Jeffrey. Harriet writes children's books and helps us live. Jennifer and Jeffrey go to school. Sometimes with us are my three children, Sandy, Tom, and Michael, astonishing sparks of myself with their own growing biographies. Sometimes with us too is my first wife, Maria, whose friendliness with Harriet and me seems to worry some people. There has been trouble in this house, and death, but now its pulse is firm and steady.

Out back, under snow now, are the deck I built and the grape arbor and the garden I tend in the summer until we go away. Out front are the tall trees and shrubs and the street where the children play. I imagined this house, this life once, shoveling snow from under my mother's clothesline in the Boston backyard or maybe delivering newspapers. I could not have imagined it all, but all that I daydreamed is here.

I do not play the organ any more, although sometimes I sing. When I finish writing I shall take my racket and play paddle tennis. I play well, and it becomes more important as I age. My father is dead, though not in me. I shall not live this long again. Next Sunday, if I have time, I shall bake more bread.

My story, like yours, is not in my condition but in the passage. That I have not told you, even the part I understand. But these conditions, too, will change, as surely as did 1953. I feel stronger for the passage ahead. I hope you do too.[8]

Throughout our Scarsdale years Harriet and I maintained a partnership in which she nurtured family and friends with help from me, and I led the school district with invaluable help from her. The house at 10 Claremont Road in Scarsdale provided a safe harbor for the busy comings and goings of the family inside. It is a lovely house: a 1917 colonial with five bedrooms, an ample living room with a serious fireplace, a dining room with a faux Tiffany chandelier taken with permission from my childhood home in Roslindale, a family room we built off the kitchen, and a cellar workbench for me. We bought it when we were married in 1973, when it was still possible for a civil servant to afford a home. We still live in it, more than forty years later.

The work of my hands is everywhere upon it. In our first years here money was tight, mostly because we were paying college tuitions for my children. If home improvements were needed, I would make them. I have painted and/or wallpapered each and every room in this house at least three or four times. I tiled the kitchen floor. I fixed the plumbing that goes from the cellar into the yard, sweating joints and cutting piping as needed. I installed the electric light that shines on the stairs outside by the street, and with the help of my son Tommy and two of his college-age friends, I re-shingled the roof. There is no nook or cranny on which I have not put my hands.

Over the years 10 Claremont Road has been a gathering place for ever-widening and overlapping circles of friends. There are past and present school board members, teachers and administrators, active citizens, parents, children, children's parents, and paddle tennis players. The events we've held have been as varied as the participants: dinner parties, cocktail parties, receptions, holidays, births, and even deaths. We've had scotch by the fireside in the winter, vodka and tonics on the rear deck in the summer, a Chaucer party where participants came dressed as Canterbury pilgrims and read their poems, and even a World War II party to honor friends who fought. We dressed in WWII garb and read Churchillian prose and letters from reporters, soldiers, all of which was gathered by Harriet. As the years passed, our circles grew wider. Together with our friends we wove a social tapestry that enriched our lives and tied us to the community, an asset in such a lively school district.

Paddle tennis and regular tennis also became a big part of my social life during my Scarsdale years. I'm almost embarrassed to tell you how big a part of my life it was. During the fall and winter the game was paddle;

Tom playing paddle tennis, 1980. Courtesy of Patricia Agre, photographer.

regular tennis was the game in the spring and summer. I played at least three or four times a week, year in and year out. We had weekday 6:30 a.m. games scheduled by the great paddle-meister, Ed Schroeder, the organizer of our two official associations: INERTA and INEPTA. INEPTA was the "International Early Paddle Tennis Association." INERTA, of course, was the "International Early Regular Tennis Association." As humorous as these organization names may be, they are real. However, the "International" label was a joke. The two groups existed only in Scarsdale. The most important rule of both groups was that the only excuse for not getting a substitute if you couldn't play was death or hospitalization.

Those guys became very important to me. We were friends off the court as well as on. Especially my paddle partner, Al "Too-Good" Wallach, with whom I won the Senior Men's Championship in all of Scarsdale two years in a row, in 1979 and 1980.

In addition to my school friends and my tennis friends there was a third circle. It had no name. It wasn't a defined group. It was more like a protozoan with a nucleus at the center and different arms reaching out. Although many of us knew each other for years and formed a core, the group never was a clique; we all had other friends. A few were old friends Harriet brought with her when we were married.

Those were good years with bad moments. Three out of four of our parents died. We went to funerals. We helped each other out. We were there for each other. We have been fortunate that we found friends who remain close to this day, friends who became family, whose children became family to us as ours did to them. They were and are the most wonderfully intelligent, caring, sane, decent people that you could possibly imagine. Sadly, a few have died. But most still surround us with great love in good times and bad. It's not that we aren't friendly with other people, but as the years go by, that core of friends has come to mean more and more. You watch them experience their lives as you experience your own.

10 Claremont Road, Scarsdale.

When I was young I didn't think much about friendship. I took it for granted. You found friends where you worked, where you studied, where you horsed around, and it seemed they would always be there. You didn't invest much in it. But I have come to realize that the linking of one's self to others is a strong cord. It has helped me to survive many difficult times.

When you're the superintendent of schools in a small town, the membrane between public life and private life is highly permeable. I had conversations on the paddle court with people whose children were having problems, or at the dry cleaners where an angry mother would complain about behavior on the three o'clock bus. That never bothered me. In fact, I rather liked it. I never considered it an intrusion.

Occasionally, an agitated parent would call me at home. One acquaintance called at about 11:30 p.m. on a Sunday night because the quality of his sixth-grade daughter's math homework was not up to snuff and might prevent her from taking an AP course in the high school. I thought that was beyond the pale, and pointed out to him that nobody was bleeding because of the quality of her math homework, particularly at 11:30 p.m. on a Sunday night. But that kind of thing was rare.

Scarsdale is the quintessential wealthy suburb. Its small population (17,500) is sheltered by comfortable homes, flourishing gardens, and healthy trees. Its commercial enterprises are few and limited to those that provide the necessities: there's a wine cellar, a cheese shop, three jewelry stores, etc. Its inhabitants are businessmen, lawyers, bankers, and money-makers easily able to support their families and provide for teachers who prepare students for the elite colleges they will attend. Indeed, community members often say that education is their only industry. Scarsdale has seven public schools: five elementary schools, a middle school, and a high school. To the external observer, these schools are excellent. Students are capable and eager to learn, teachers are intelligent and hard-working, management is on top of things, and money is abundant and properly spent. More than ninety percent of high school seniors go on to four-year colleges, year after year. The schools are a model of what public schools could be like everywhere given adequate resources, a competent staff, and a supportive community. No blemish mars this idyllic scene.

Or so it seems. From inside, things look different. What are the consequences of striving for excellence, day in and out? What about the student, the teacher, the parent who can't seem to keep up? What is their attitude toward the school likely to be? What difficulties inevitably arise when the students with special needs lay claim to their entitlements? What do you lose when the student body and faculty is nearly one hundred percent white? In what ways and to what extent should teachers, administrators, parents, civic organizations, the Board of Education, citizens, and students themselves participate in making educational decisions? Few communities are so interested, involved, or capable. But how do you reconcile differences when everyone is smarter than everyone else, and often eager to say so?

Questions such as these have shaped much of the district's agenda over the years. I am proud to have been a key participant in the perennial pursuit of quality in all matters. Quality in schools is a product of the work students and teachers do, not from the work of superintendents. But even superintendents should have their day in court. Here are thumbnail sketches of ten achievements I am proud of:

1) We kept school well. This may be the most important and least remarkable of all our achievements. We notice least what we see most, precisely because keeping school is so quietly ubiquitous. Consider these small daily miracles: early in the morning the busses crisscross our streets and pull into their designated areas, 5000 children shuffle themselves into order and settle down in their assigned classrooms, and hundreds of teachers meet them and begin instruction. In the next few hours thousands of

decisions will be made and actions will be taken to promote sound teaching and learning. And so it goes, day after day, week after week, month after month, year after year. This doesn't happen by accident. Organizations tend to deteriorate without a guiding hand. Scarsdale deserves high marks for making the high quality of its educational programs a quiet commonplace.

2) For years kindergarten was a half-day program, with a callback feature that provided time for small groups of children to be with the teacher some afternoons. The children who were not called back that day would stay at home. By 1971 a substantial number of parents, chiefly working mothers, were lobbying for a full-day kindergarten program. An approximately equal number of stay-at-home parents argued for the status quo.

The issue was researched and debated for weeks. Each side brought in consultants to buttress their arguments. At one point I suggested that parents be allowed to choose whether their child would attend in the afternoon or not. That way everyone would get what he or she wants, or so I thought. "No way," said the stay-home mothers. "If you offer an all-day program we will have to send our children to it. Otherwise our children will fall behind. Welcome to Scarsdale, Mr. Superintendent." Eventually we established a full-day program, and all the children came.

3) The women's rights movement had a significant effect on the Scarsdale schools. The '70s and '80s saw sea changes in women's roles. Groups of parents fought the half-day kindergarten and the long-standing policy of sending elementary school children home for lunch. The attitudes of women were shifting. Groups of women came to my office, to board meetings, and to PTA meetings and said, "We're not always at home at noon when the kids have lunch. We think you should let the kids eat in school." Others found lunch at home with their kids a good experience and wanted to keep things the way they had been. For a while, I felt that my job was to be the bridge between two warring factions of women. Some acted as if they believed a woman's place was in the home, damn it, and

you should be there with the cookies baking when the child comes home at noon. Other women were off to work, or school, or lunch with a friend and felt they were being put down by innuendo or told outright that they were not worthy as mothers if they weren't home at noon to give their children lunch.

It was tricky to bring those two groups together, but we did, and eventually, we developed a lunch program that met everybody's satisfaction, more or less. Parents who wanted their children to eat lunch in school brought their lunch. Parents who wanted their children to come home for lunch could make that choice. It was a simple solution, but it took time to bring everyone to it.

4) A few years later, I helped a group of women establish a childcare center called Kids Base, making Scarsdale even more desirable to young families buying homes in the district. The program provides supervision and recreational activity for children whose parents are working in the early morning and/or the late afternoon. The venture is private; no public funds are involved.

5) Public Law 94-142, the Education of All Handicapped Children Act, was passed by the United States Congress in 1975, setting in motion a train of procedural regulations that schools must follow in order to provide an appropriate education for students with handicapping conditions. Previously, New York State school districts could refuse handicapped children entrance to their schools if there were no appropriate education program for the child. Under the new law, school districts were required to develop appropriate programs for all but the most severely handicapped. The programs were to be given in the least restrictive environment, at public expense. It took several years to interpret the regulations and put them fully to effect.

In some districts, bad feelings developed between parents and boards of education as new demands met old resistance. In Scarsdale, the board, the staff, and the parents worked together for a common cause. A group of parents formed an organization called SOLD (Scarsdale Organization for Learning Disabilities) and worked as a group to bring the learning-disabled children back to the Scarsdale schools with help from the district. We established learning centers within the schools and staffed the centers with teachers trained in teaching children with learning disabilities. Not only did we bring the learning-disabled children home, but we also integrated them into the schools with their neighbors. In doing so, we taught all the children that everyone is different, with some of us needing more help than others.

I remember a child who was physically handicapped as a result of cerebral palsy. She was confined to a wheelchair. No one had ever attended our schools in a wheelchair. Rather extraordinary when we think about it today! In any event, she conveniently attended the Heathcote School, which has only one floor. The teachers were nervous about her attendance, but the child flourished, and is a lawyer today.

6) The Scarsdale Alternative School opened in 1972, a time when the Vietnam War was still raging, a time of student rebellion and political upheaval. It remains open in 2014, forty-two years later—one of my proudest achievements. What began as an outlet for student anger against the war turned out to be a model of progressive education. It also helped to shape the "small schools" movement of recent years. Anxious parents have occasionally asked me, "Why are you trying something new when what we want is the status quo?" My reply is that in any organization that is alive and growing, the only way to preserve the status quo is through progressive change.

7) Throughout the sixteen years of my stewardship in office, temporary bulges and shortages in elementary and middle school enrollment posed problems for the school administration. At times, if no remedy were applied, some schools would have been overcrowded while others had empty classrooms. The board's goal was to place the students where there was room for them, while disrupting as few students as possible.

One of our elementary schools (the Edgewood School) was crowded. Fifth grade pupils were assigned to a temporary classroom on the school playground. Parents were angry. The board and I proposed a redistricting whereby some forty to fifty pupils from Edgewood would be transferred to the abutting school attendance area (Fox Meadow). We explained that the schools were similar, the distances short, and the portable classroom would no longer be needed. Further, there would be a net savings to taxpayers. But the parents said, "No way."

The parents had deeply-felt reasons for resisting the move, and they made their case with sometimes fiendish ingenuity. One father appeared at a meeting carrying a small American flag and announcing his defense of "the territorial integrity of the Edgewood attendance area." He was serious.

After numerous meetings, letters, op-ed pieces, telephone calls, and chance discussions at the grocery store, the board went ahead with its plan. The parents remained angry, in some cases, for years. One big reason for the resistance may have been a long-standing practice among Scarsdale real estate agents to guide Jewish clients to Fox Meadow, and Christian clients to Edgewood. The practice had been discontinued, but its effects remained. Who knows how much, if any, this segregated arrangement influenced the complaining Edgewood parents? The matter was never raised in public. Never. And the children who changed districts did just fine.

8) About two years before my arrival in Scarsdale, the New York State Legislature enacted the Public Employment Act, known colloquially as the Taylor Law. The law forbids strikes by public employees and requires employers and employees to engage in a process of collective bargaining to determine terms and conditions of employment. Boards of education and teachers' union representatives had not yet developed procedures and norms to help them with the new requirements when the law took effect.

In many districts the going was rough. Some board members who were familiar with boards in the private sector were annoyed by it. Others were angered, even resentful. Some teachers were deliberately disruptive to the bargaining, seeing the process as a place to express anger they had accumulated over many years. Often, boards and teachers saw one another as enemies, not as partners.

I made changing this relationship one of my top priorities. I met with union officials once a week, to discuss both current problems and long-term relationships. I invited them to some of my administrative council meetings. I taught a course (The Hidden Curriculum) in a professional development program run by Scarsdale teachers, for Scarsdale teachers. And I made sure that each of my many talks and conversations with members of the staff and community would instill pride in our school system.

Over the next few years, as teachers came to trust me, the management/labor relationship indeed became a partnership. In my view the current efforts in some states to strip teachers of their collective bargaining rights are not only unfair to the teachers, they are bad for the schools.

9) I'm proud that we managed money well. People think of Scarsdale as wealthy, and as the world goes, so it is. But the fact is that for most of the sixteen years that I was superintendent, the per pupil expenditure in Scarsdale was about at the median for the forty-plus school districts in Westchester and Putnam Counties. In fairness, most of our debt service had been paid off, and we didn't have large transportation expenses. Nevertheless, per pupil expenditure was about average, and we were certainly getting better than average results.

10) In the late 1970s the Levittown, Long Island school district led a group of property-poor school districts—including New York City and four other large city school districts—in the lawsuit, *Levittown v. Nyquist*, challenging New York State's system of financing education. The plaintiffs argued that the existing system of financial aid was not constitutional. They noted the disparity of per pupil expenditure between the poorer districts and the wealthier districts. Not only did the plaintiffs want more state aid for the poorer districts, they also wanted a spending cap on all local districts. In other words, they wanted the state to limit spending in districts

like Scarsdale, Great Neck, and other wealthy districts. As a result, districts would be limited in the amount they would be able to tax their own citizens as well as the amount they would be able to spend on their students' education. I felt this would be terribly unfair to our students, as well as generally detrimental to the state of education across the state.

I organized a group of suburban districts. We engaged an attorney steeped in constitutional law and sought standing as amicus (friend of the court). The court granted our petition. We submitted a brief and participated in oral argument.

In 1982, the court rejected plaintiff Levittown's appeal. The ruling acknowledged that although there were substantial inequities in funding education, New York's state constitution does not require equality in funding for education. The court added that the state constitution does, however, entitle all students to a "sound basic education." The Levittown case was a precursor to the more recent Campaign for Fiscal Equity case in which I participated when I was commissioner and will be described in the Albany section.

New York State law requires that residents of school districts approve an annual budget. Among other requirements is a formal hearing held each May. Citizens receive copies of the budget more than two weeks prior to the event. The board of education presides over the meeting, and approximately two hundred taxpayers and the local press make it an important event in the life of the district.

At a typical meeting in Scarsdale, five or six particularly dedicated critics invariably do their homework and come well-prepared to shoot down any changes requested by the board and superintendent. Among these was a self-appointed chief critic named Robert Hackett.

By the time I was appointed superintendent, Mr. Hackett had a well-established reputation as someone who would excoriate the board and the staff. He often called them out as arrogant, evasive, and even incompetent. Year after year the attacks would be made, and superintendents would quiver when we reached the month of May. Yet, I felt he played an important role in the democratic process, and I valued his participation, even though we rarely agreed.

There came a year when I realized that Mr. Hackett had not made his annual appearance. I picked up the telephone and called him. How was he, I wanted to know.

"Fine," he answered. "What do you want?"

I asked if he was planning to attend the annual budget meeting.

"No," he replied. His wife had died and he was living alone in his Scarsdale house. His legs were bad. He didn't drive anymore.

I expressed my commiseration. "I'll tell you what. I'll come over to your house on the night of the meeting and drop you off at the middle school, where the meeting will be held."

He agreed. On the night of the meeting I knocked on his door and he was there, standing in his stocking feet and holding two shoes in one hand. I helped him put on his shoes. He carried a copy of the budget in one hand and took my arm with the other. We walked together to my car. I drove to the middle school and saw that he was appropriately seated in the auditorium.

About halfway through the hearing he raised his hand to ask for the floor. The board president granted his request, while trembling before the coming onslaught. Bob Hackett, whatever else may be said about him, had done his homework. He saw what was wrong with both the big picture and petty details. He excoriated us and called us arrogant, evasive, and deceitful. He accepted the praise of his supporters, then shouted out, "Vote that budget down," and sat down.

When the meeting was over, I said good night to everyone and drove Bob home. We didn't talk. I took him to his bedroom and helped him to take his shoes off. Finally he said, "Thank you."

I said, "No problem."

He went to bed satisfied that he had exposed us for the charlatans we were. I slept well, knowing I had done a good thing.

Scarsdale works because it is a community. It is not only a place, but a state of mind. It has its own history, traditions, legends, culture, and even diet. The school district and village lines are nearly coterminous. To paraphrase Gertrude Stein, there is a there, there.

All parties share the same goal: success through education. Students are motivated to do well in school because their futures depend upon it. Parents not only preach the gospel of success, they define it in the work they do. Taxpayers (hopefully) recognize that the checks they write support the value of the homes they live in. Whether spoken aloud or quietly assumed, the message is clear: "Success through education!"

And what an honor it is to be among the leaders of such an enterprise! I felt this honor every year at our high school graduation ceremony. The students, wearing caps and gowns, brimmed with joy and energy, giddy with the knowledge that they were taking a long leap forward into independence and adulthood. The parents, grandparents, and the friends came from all over, smiling at everything and wearing their Sunday best. One such graduation was particularly memorable. The assistant superintendent of business had the custodians paint the outdoor bleachers green two days before graduation. Naturally, the paint didn't dry thoroughly. When they got back up, the audience discovered their pants and dresses were striped with green: everyone's Sunday best covered in wet paint. Mimi's Cleaners never had it so good. Dozens of people berated me for not exercising good judgment. I took the heat, but I ask you: what was I supposed to do, tell the assistant superintendent to be sure not to paint the bleachers green two days before graduation?

As I said, people came from all over. This was not only a high school event, it was a family and community event. The students were not graduating from the high school alone. They were graduating from the Edgewood, Fox Meadow, Greenacres, Heathcote, and Quaker Ridge elementary and middle schools as well. The adults were graduating along with them, marking their own passage of time.

I can feel it now. I rise from my chair and walk across the stage to the podium, carefully taking my speech from my jacket. We are outdoors at the high school, in a courtyard opposite the baseball diamond. Behind me are the principals, teacher leaders, board of education members, and other notables. On one side is the student band, which has just finished playing Elgar's graduation hymn. On the other side are the students' parents, grandparents, relatives, and friends. Before me, sitting on gray metal folding chairs, are the students, about to become graduates. Beyond them, sitting on the wooden bleachers so recently painted green, are the remaining adults and a straggle of young teenagers sitting on the grass or riding their bicycles. I grasp the podium with two hands and look out at the students, running my eyes up and down the rows so as not to miss anyone I know. I know a good many, I think. The number tends to vary from year to year. I am, after all, a superintendent, no longer a classroom teacher. I raise my head and gaze beyond the bleachers to the ball field and the library with its pond and fir trees, and then further out to a late June sky where a gathering storm can be felt as much as seen. I am awed by it all. I am humbled to be the person whose task is to bring this all together: to connect the students, parents, and grandparents with the community of Scarsdale and the larger communities of space and time that stretch out beyond the fir trees and the pond with my words. I turn a page and begin to speak.

Nothing stays the same. We change, boards of education change, communities change. During the years I was in Scarsdale, public behavior began to change. There was a dramatic decline in public civility during my Scarsdale years. It may have been the legacy of Vietnam. It may have been the legacy of Watergate. It may just have been the times in general. I don't know why, but people were not only less polite in public sessions, they were more arrogant. They were more demanding. They would insult you without even knowing that they were insulting you. They were oblivious to it. They would act as if you were stupid and everybody knew it, and you certainly should have been kind enough to tell the truth.

I think it's very sad. Perhaps because I was a public servant, the attitude rankled me. You know you're breaking your hump. You know you're not perfect to begin with, so you're never going to get everything right. There is always going to be something wrong. I used to say to people, I don't mind it. I don't like it, but I can tolerate it when people question my judgment or my capacity. But it bothers me when they question my good faith. All I want is to do this right. There was more and more of that as time went on. It's partly what made it time, eventually, to leave.

When Gordon Ambach, my predecessor as commissioner of education in New York State, announced he was leaving, I set out to get the job. This was the only time I sought a job. I didn't do that in Scarsdale. I didn't do it in Great Neck. But I set out to get the commissionership. I worked at it. I cultivated regents. I wrote and published papers. I asked people to recommend me. I spoke at statewide PTA and Teachers' Union meetings, as well as other educational organizations. I made myself a presence.

However, as good as the Scarsdale years were, something mysterious began to happen about two years before I left. I realized that the sole of my left foot was becoming numb. It felt as if I had a block of wood on the bottom of my foot. I told Harriet about it but didn't worry too much. I wasn't one to go to the doctor and as I mentioned before, I had very little time. Perhaps I delayed seeing a physician because I was afraid of what I would find out.

Finally, I saw my internist who referred me to a neurologist. I don't know when I began to worry about Lou Gehrig's disease, but I know it was in the back of my mind early on. My symptom was called "peripheral neuropathy." The neurologist's diagnosis was spinal stenosis. I kept my running, paddle tennis, and tennis up, and avoided thinking about what I sensed might be coming. My focus was on Albany.

CHAPTER 6

Albany

"The American dilemma need not become the American tragedy. We have it within our power to make of this continuing American experiment a model of the richness that diversity can bring. In these ways we are already showing others how to live. By embracing our diversity, by all of us learning more about each others' differences, accepting them, and moving on to emphasize our common humanity, our shared values, and our common destiny, we can show other societies in this teeming global village how to flourish in a world that suddenly shrank before differences among tribes were eroded."

—Thomas Sobol, *Teachers College Record*, 1993[9]

Although diverse people have always sought refuge in the United States, they have not always been welcome. Throughout our history, populations have left their countries to emigrate to our nation. Those who are already citizens have often expected immigrants to be part of the American melting pot, to reject their culture and adopt ours as quickly as possible.

Population projections in the 1980s indicated schools would have a more diverse population than ever before in the history of the country. Many of the new immigrants were not buying into the old "melting pot" paradigm. Cheaper travel and communications helped many people to visit and connect with their country of origin more often, and some people began holding onto their customs. Some politicians termed the new paradigm a mosaic: many differences uniting to make one nation, but the melting-pot metaphor remained an ideal for many people. At the same time the civil rights movement of the 1960s and 1970s continued to make advances in the 1980s. People of color believed it was time to claim their rightful role in the nation's history. They felt they had been anonymous too long. The reaction to my appointment as New York State Commissioner of Education by people of color was a reflection of the times. Throughout the spring of 1987, the newspapers reflected the black and Hispanic community's negative feelings about the appointment.

Nevertheless, the clock ticked on.

Some weeks after my appointment by the Board of Regents, Chancellor Marty Barell met with Harriet and me about the commissioner's residence in Albany. Marty was a lovely man. The residence was a grand place. It had twenty-six rooms. There were either six bathrooms and seven fireplaces, or six fireplaces and seven bathrooms. I can't remember which. It was set on nine cultivated acres with trees, a lilac walk, formal gardens, stone walls, and a gazebo. "What a wonderful opportunity to entertain there," said the chancellor. "The regents expect you to live there."

Harriet was skeptical about the job. She was not comfortable with the idea of leaving Scarsdale. Scarsdale was well-known, secure, and comfortable. Our friends were there. The kids were there. She never quite said so, but I came to believe she thought I was being vain to want the job and that I was upsetting the apple cart. She said that the press would be different from what I had experienced in Scarsdale. They would be critical as a matter of course, and that would be hard on me. She turned out to be correct about the press, unfortunately. One exception was *The New York Times*, which had excellent reporters who wrote what actually happened. I appreciated their coverage as well as the access I had to public television and radio, both of which gave me a broader opportunity to talk with the public about what we were trying to do.

Harriet raised a great many questions and, in her inimitable style, made sure that I found the answers. I called Gordon Ambach, my predecessor, to get some of the information I needed to decide whether to take the job. I wanted to know how much traveling he did and what kind of expense account the regents would authorize. Those were questions that I would never have asked the regents in a million years. It's just not in me. I'm grateful to have been able to talk to Gordon about much of that.

Gordon and his wife Lucy were kind enough to invite us to see the residence. We visited on a beautiful day in early April. They took us all around the nine acres and the twenty-six rooms. After our tour we thanked them and got in the car for the drive back to Scarsdale. We were silent as we drove out the long circular driveway through the stately chestnut trees and hemlocks. I chanced a sidelong glance at my wife and knew that I was in deep trouble. Through tears, she said, "It's not the kind of political statement you ought to be making. You're supposed to be improving the lives of poor minority kids who are getting the short end of the stick. It's just plain wrong for you to ensconce yourself in a place like this. You've already been criticized for being wealthy and out of touch and you haven't even started the job. Why don't you go tell the regents that?"

After fourteen years of marriage, Harriet and I felt the same about many things. The residence in Albany was one of them. I had been thinking the same things while on our tour. So I expressed my concerns with the Regents.

I didn't convene a meeting of the entire board. By then I knew Marty and Vice Chancellor Carballada well enough to approach them individually.

I was aware that I might be causing them difficulty, but I went ahead and argued my case as forcefully as I could. I felt living in the residence would be a political error. There was enough trouble from the black caucus with my appointment, and this would only give them more ammunition to argue that I was privileged and uncommitted to equality. Marty explained that the residence was a valuable resource for the Education Department. The regents used it to bring education groups and politically-oriented groups together. They had no other venue in which to do that. The vice chancellor added that college presidents have houses and use them to good effect, and there is no reason why the president of the University of the State of New York (the accrediting and licensing organization for the State Education Department, and which the Commissioner presides over) shouldn't have that too. It was clear to me that short of drawing a line in the sand and saying, "I'm not going to take the job if we have to live there," we'd be moving to the residence in Albany. And that was a step I was simply not prepared to take. I would have to tell Harriet my mission failed. I delivered the news in an expensive Italian restaurant in New York City. People stared at us as tears rolled down Harriet's face. Here I was, explaining that we would have to move into one of the most opulent mansions in upstate New York, and the other patrons probably thought I was breaking up with her.

As I mentioned before, one of the first things I did was appoint four task forces: one to address high school dropouts, one to look at the over-representation of black males in special education classes, one to address the underrepresentation of minorities on the State Education Department staff, and one to review the state's curriculum guides concerning minority people.

The task force studying the state curriculum guides titled their report *A Curriculum of Inclusion*. Their response reflected the feelings of many blacks and Hispanics about the education system in the 1980s. As I said many times to many people, "If you ask people who aren't used to being asked how they feel about something, they are going to tell you."

I'm sure many people think I shouldn't have even asked, but I still believe it was the right thing to do. Maybe it wasn't the right time but I didn't choose the time, it chose me.

The task force that wrote *A Curriculum of Inclusion* was not asked to write a curriculum, nor did they. The task force members, all distinguished members of their respective fields, had reviewed the state's curriculum guides and, finding many problems, had sounded an alarm. Now we needed a group of professional specialists to advise and guide us on the development of a new curriculum. After consulting with teachers and experts throughout the country, the Board of Regents created the Social Studies Syllabus Review and Development Committee. This committee consisted of twenty-four eminent scholars and teachers in history and other social studies representing a variety of viewpoints and racial/ethnic backgrounds. There were eighteen members: Kermit Ackley, Daniel Berman, Barbara Bernard, Linda Bierman, Lloyd Bromberg, Mary Carter, Claire F. Deloria, Lloyd Elm, William Fetsko, Nathan Glazer, Michael Hooper, Kenneth Jackson, Jorge Klor de Alva, Kathy Kornblith, Ali Mazrui, Virginia Sanchez Korrol, Susan Sagor, and in a special "consulting" role, Arthur Schlesinger Jr. The committee's charge was to examine the state syllabi and to recommend changes in them and in the teaching of them that would promote students' understanding of one another, our culture, and the world.

Although we had moved to Albany, we kept our house in Scarsdale. Harriet's father lived in Eastchester, ten minutes away, and on the weekends Harriet would go home. She'd make dinners for her father that he could use during the week. Jeffrey, Harriet's twenty-one-year-old son was working nearby. He lived in our house and was on call should his grandfather need help. Harriet continued to lead her writing workshop but changed it from Thursdays to Monday mornings.

We had few "typical" weeks since my schedule was constantly changing. But I would often leave early on Sunday afternoons to go to Albany alone, taking my amply packed briefcases with me. I would work in the residence that night to get ready for Monday morning, and Harriet would come up on Monday night. Unless I was traveling around the state or working in New York City (which was often the case), we would spend the week in Albany and then each of us would travel back to Scarsdale on Friday. Harriet always went home earlier than I did and traveled with our black lab Patra, who made the local newspaper. A reporter interviewed Harriet and thought her commute with Patra deserved a photo of her and Harriet in the car. We both loved Patra, but sometimes she was an embarrassment. A wanderer, she often brought garbage home to us from our neighbors, Siena College. The well-tended lawn of the residence didn't deserve McDonald's refuse so Harriet checked the grounds when Patra returned from a day out.

We paid a nominal rent for the Albany residence, of course. We never made use of all twenty-six rooms. We lived in just four rooms. We wallpapered the kitchen to lighten it up, and there was a little room off the kitchen that had a television set, a computer, and Harriet's personal belongings. When it was just the two of us or when we were with friends, we ate our meals in that little room. In fact, we spent most of our waking time at the residence in that room. We ate breakfast there and read or watched tv in the evenings. But other than the kitchen, that little room off the kitchen, our bedroom, and a room that had a television set next to our bedroom, the house remained unused. Harriet did do some necessary remodeling. She took down the drapes and put lace curtains everywhere, she took up the wall-to-wall carpeting, and she generally made the house more welcoming to official and unofficial guests. But the Albany residence was not a home and it had a lonely feel to it. It felt especially lonely when Harriet was not there, and she felt it during the day when I was working. The graceful circular staircase, the large dining room, the sunken living room, and the long upstairs hallway with all the bedrooms made for a lot of empty space. The third floor with its smaller bedrooms and the basement almost felt haunted, and for a long time we avoided them.

Our home in Scarsdale had radiated activity. Harriet's kids grew up there, my kids came and went, friends often dropped in. Our yard was small, so we were close to our neighbors. It felt like there were always people around.

Through work with the Actors Shakespeare Company, which Harriet's daughter had helped start, and her membership on the Albany Arts Commission, Harriet met a number of interesting people, including nuns and priests who worked with the homeless, a woman who ran a drug treatment center, and the newspaper editor and his wife—all of whom became guests at the residence. Gradually, Harriet found a way to fill up the house and bring it to life. We invited members of the press to have dinner with *The New York Times* columnist Anna Quindlen after she gave a speech for The New York Preservation Archive Project about the search for local newspapers from people's attics and basements. Anna stayed over as well.

We hung elementary and junior high school student art in the living and dining rooms, and the kids would come with their parents and their art teachers for a viewing and celebration. These felt like important events, and there would be ice cream afterward. Groups of teachers would visit when they were having meetings in Albany. We told them the house was theirs as well as ours.

Throughout this time both my feet had become numb and I could feel a burning on the skin of my legs. I was losing my balance. I had stopped running or playing paddle tennis. I was referred to a neurosurgeon who, after some tests, told me I didn't have spinal stenosis. The surgeon recommended I go for a complete neurological workup. My doctor's visits, tests, and procedures were squeezed into time I didn't feel I had, but I kept making appointments because it was clear that something terrible was happening to me. No one was sure exactly what. I didn't have Lou Gehrig's disease. I didn't have Lyme disease. I didn't have MS. No one had a diagnosis, but my doctors recommended physical therapy, so I tried to fit that into my already tight schedule.

My balance got worse. If I could walk next to a wall I was OK. Otherwise, Harriet told me, I looked like I was drunk. She recommended I get a cane. I wrote a memo to the regents about my situation and assured them that it wouldn't interfere with my work. Eventually, walking for more than a block became impossible, and I still had no diagnosis. As involved in my work as I was, as much as we entertained, there was a nagging uncertainty at the back of my mind. Where was this going? How would it end? I had already lost the ability to play tennis and paddle tennis. Walking, even with the help of a cane was difficult, particularly for long distances. What else would I lose?

It took a few years for the Social Studies Syllabus Review and Development Committee to prepare their report. In 1988, three years before the committee completed its work, I started working on *A New Compact for Learning*. These two initiatives were taking place at the same time and I was immersed in both.

In June 1991, the Social Studies Committee submitted its report: *One Nation, Many Peoples: A Declaration of Cultural Independence*. The report was more scholarly in tone and illustration than its predecessor, although the central message was much the same. The committee recommended that the present New York State social studies syllabi be revised to provide more opportunities for students to learn from multiple perspectives and to remove language that may be interpreted as racist or sexist. The report included as well a statement of sound principles for teaching and learning to guide teachers in implementing these changes.

What we had before us was still an advisory report, not an official recommendation by the commissioner or a policy decision by the Board of Regents. During the next few weeks, I wrote and submitted my own recommendations to the regents, adopting most of the report's substance, incorporating the gist of dissenting opinions, and casting the whole thing in my own language.

In making my recommendations to the Board, I proposed a curriculum:

[T]hat will tell more of the truth about more of our history to all of our children. It is a curriculum based on fact, faithful to historical proportion, and grounded in the democratic and moral values of our common American culture. It is a curriculum that informs young people fully of the ideals and struggles that have shaped our nation, that gives young people a reason for believing they have a stake in its success, and that prepares young people to participate effectively in an increasingly diverse society and an increasingly shrinking world.

If we are to have such a curriculum, there are two things we must do. First, as the report *One Nation, Many Peoples* maintains: "Special attention will need to be given to those values, characteristics, and traditions which we share in common. Our children must be grounded in the American ideals and values that are the envy of so much of the world: the rule of law, freedom of speech, minority rights, tolerance of dissent, respect for individuals, and more. They must know the facts of our history and understand the trends of our history and be familiar with the great documents of our history. Whatever their background, they must understand themselves to be Americans, fully participant in the ongoing American experiment, sharing a common American destiny. We must teach our common culture."

The second thing we must do is make sure that all of us Americans are included. Without "making up facts" or "rewriting history" we must tell the story of all the major groups that comprise American society today. The United States of America is not only a unique democracy; it is one of the most ethnically diverse countries on earth. In order to understand one another, we must come to know each other. We must be careful, as Professor Glazer has warned, not to make ethnic groups more rigid or permanent than they are. But so long as they have relevance for so many of our people, their story, as part of the American story, must be told.

Social studies syllabi should be written so as to reflect these truths. Our history and the story of our many peoples must reflect not only our achievements, but our shortcomings; not only our triumphs, but our pain; and not only our failures, but our successes and ideals. This is not to say that all cultures or civilizations are equal; but it is to say that students are capable of understanding the complexity of human nature and the human experience, and an education that does not help them do so sells them short.[10]

The regents approved our recommendations, which guided the review-and-revision process that followed. Later, they were incorporated into the new standards-setting project: an initiative involving all academic subjects of study including social studies. By 1995 when I was leaving Albany, the project was nearly completed.

We had a wonderful party at the residence after the committee members had completed their work. They had worked well as a group and were delighted to celebrate together. After dinner, Lloyd Elm, a Native American from Buffalo, cleared his throat and asked us to forgive him for interrupting our thoughts, and then recited a prayer handed down from his father, and his father's father before him, "going back through history to before the white man landed on our shores." The rest of the committee members were held in rapt attention. We were all multiculturalists, that day.

Harriet was doing everything she could to make my life better. She supported my work and created a positive social life for us in Albany. Before long she became what I called "the queen of Albany." Friends in Scarsdale teased her about "her staff." She came to enjoy having a caterer, a gardening staff, and people she could call when the sink got stopped up, the heat didn't work, or if she saw a mouse. She enjoyed meeting famous people and inviting them over for dinner, especially William Kennedy, the author of *Ironweed*.

During our years in Scarsdale, we had had a large social life. It was nothing elaborate, but we hosted many parties and dinners with others at the spur of the moment, so it was not difficult to begin entertaining in Albany. Harriet threw wonderful parties. Every Christmas, for instance, we hosted a big event for the Board of Regents. Harriet always made sure to seat Regent Carballada next to her. He was the vice chancellor when I became commissioner but later became chancellor. Harriet was fond of him and found him a great dinner partner.

She was good at bringing different groups together, so we would often invite state legislators, government employees, and people from varying economic backgrounds. Both Harriet and I believe in diversity.

Neither the Board of Regents nor I was riding on a long crescendo of acclaim during those years. From the time *A Curriculum of Inclusion* first appeared, much of the press and many people in public life and academia assaulted my motives, my plans, my intelligence, even my good faith. *Time* magazine wrote, "American kids are getting a new—and divisive—view of Thomas Jefferson, Thanksgiving, and the Fourth of July."

The Wall Street Journal, in an article called "Curriculum of Diversion," opined that "little is likely to be accomplished until educators stop chasing the latest fad and get back to the basics." *The New Republic*, under the heading "Mr. Sobol's Planet," wrote, "What this report subtly does is degrade the notion of factual truth in the American story."[11] This continued to the end of my term. Many journalists had decided I was the devil and no matter what I said or did, the devil I was to be. I continued to press for a more multicultural curriculum with mixed results.

As the years passed and we met more Albanians, I came to find Albany interesting. Forming the bedrock layer are the native Albanians, the people who used to work in the General Electric factory in Schenectady or the Hudson River waterfront when there was an operating port. Railroad workers and heavy industry employees tended to be Irish Catholic, although there's a good number of Italian families among them and some of German ancestry. Some families have lived in the area for generations.

Many people from those families now hold low-level positions in government. They are custodians, secretarial staff, postal clerks, and truck drivers. The whole downstairs infrastructure of the government is maintained by those folks in the bedrock Albany families.

There is also still a privileged layer of Albany society, some descended from Dutch families. These are the people who own the factories and used to own the railroads. Their children attend private schools and they run the cultural and arts organizations. Then, of course, there are the people in the government agencies. These are the bureaucrats and the legislators, most of them not from Albany, and most of them transient.

Did we like Albany? We didn't dislike it. We liked certain things and we certainly met interesting people, but it never felt like home. If you have been in and you are now out, it must be a pretty dismal place to be, because who gets invited where depends a lot on who's in and who isn't. While you can carve out a life around that, it seems to me that once you've done it and it's over, it's time to go. You don't belong there anymore.

In a way, during those years, I belonged to New York State more than to Albany. In fact, I used to tell people that you could blindfold me and put me in front of an audience in any major area in the state, and within five minutes of discussion I could tell you where I was. I still believe that. It didn't have much to do with accents. It had to do with people's demeanor, their point of view on certain issues, their tone, and the way members of the audience related to me. There were parts of the job that I found very trying. This life that I was living—constantly working, constantly in the public eye, constantly meeting new and different people, constantly finding little time for family and friends—it was an emotional roller coaster, with great highs but dismal lows. The job was as exciting, but it was also eating me up.

Once I had been in Albany for two or three years, Harriet had me keep an informal chart of the kind of day I had had. I rated each day one through five. Five was terrific: what a wonderful day! One was a bummer. Most of the days in the middle of my eight years ranked a three or four, with a generous sprinkling of fives. Not bad!

I often think back to one particular morning in September 1988. It had been a year and some months since I became commissioner. Much of that year had been spent dousing fires from the state's social studies program. Nevertheless, I had carved out time to visit communities all over the state. I wanted to meet people, and I wanted people to meet me. I wanted to know what the general concerns about children's education were. The state is large and the people varied, but three big problems emerged. These were the dropout rate, the growing achievement gap between affluent white students and poor students of color, and the accelerating rate at which the world and technology were changing.

On this particular morning Kate Reilly, my secretary, poked her head in the tall oak doorway. "Good morning, Commissioner. Should I shut the door?"

"Good morning, Kate. Yes, please, and no calls unless they're urgent."

Her red hair disappeared and the door shut with a firm thud. Keeping in mind the concerns I had heard, I started to write. I leaned back in my chair and thought about school initiatives I had led which had been successful, and what they had in common. The Village School, the Alternative School, Scarsdale's lunch program, and others came to mind. In each case,

the desire for change had come from the community. Our education reform plan had to build on what people wanted. We would have to do a lot
of listening. I prepared a summary of what I had heard on my trips around
the state, and made notes about how I thought we should proceed. At the
end of the day, I sent copies to Skip and Sam, my deputy commissioners.
I asked them to come to the residence for a 9:00 a.m. meeting. No one
would disturb us there.

The following morning was a bright autumn day. Our excitement and
energy were palpable. We wrote, we interrupted each other, we paced
around the room. Eventually we created a plan based on the concerns
and suggestions we had solicited from around the state. The seeds of my
proudest initiative, titled *A New Compact for Learning* were sown that
September day.

The next phase was the development process. We held over a dozen
hearings around the state. The meetings were open to everyone, but were
attended mostly by parents, teachers, and administrators. Skip and Sam
often came with me, and so did regents board members. Sometimes other
department staff came as well. After the hearings we would talk in the car,
on the drive back, about what we had heard. The process was arduous but
it felt right. We made drafts and changed them, edited and deleted, making
progress each time we heard people's concerns.

From 1988 until I left Albany I was working on the *Compact*. I also
was meeting with the Board of Regents, legislators, school superintendents,
teachers union leaders, and other people on a variety of issues. And then
there were my social obligations. We invited legislators and legislative
staff to dine with us. We invited people from educational organizations
and people who worked at the State Education Department. Guests at one
dinner party included both José Serrano, a Democrat from the Bronx and
the chairman of the Assembly Education Committee; and James Donovan,
a Republican from upstate and the chairman of the Senate Education
Committee. I was a little nervous, but Harriet wasn't. Assemblyman

Serrano and Senator Donovan had a great time together and perhaps the dinner helped improve their working relationship. At its September 1990 meeting, the Board of Regents voted unanimously to approve *A New Compact for Learning*, making it official state education policy. The *Compact* would become our game plan for educational reform through the 1990s. It would be an agreement among all parties to come together and do what they could to improve students' education. The *Compact* defined a new relationship between the state and local authority, one that we characterized as top-down support for bottom-up reform. The agreement was based on the principle that all children can learn. We set forth specific goals and strategies to achieve those goals, and set out to make the *Compact* a reality.

Summers were a little less hectic than the school year. Our social inroads into the city of Albany started with our kids. Harriet's daughter Jenny and her friends, John Plummer and Peter Greenberg, formed a theater group called the Actors Shakespeare Company, with a core of about eight or ten young actors. Each summer they performed Shakespeare plays free to the public in Albany's Washington Park. They also did outreach at local inner city organizations, invited kids and their families to come to the shows, received grants from NYSCA, the Newman Foundation, and contributions from individuals and local businesses to help fund their efforts. Area colleges gave them free housing and one of the corporations gave them rehearsal space.

Their audiences grew and the performances became an important piece of Albany's summer scene. Shows were performed on a wooden stage built by the company. One year a homeless family took up residence under the stage. The actors were too sympathetic to ask them to vacate the premises. But during a performance of *Comedy of Errors*, the audience suddenly heard a loud knocking from the stage floor. Apparently the noise was too loud for the inhabitants down under who were expressing their annoyance.

It was fun to go down to the park on a summer night, spread a blanket out, have a picnic supper, and wait for the show to begin while the actors walked among the crowd warming up. All of that was very pleasant. Harriet applied for and got 501C3 (nonprofit) status for the company, and in the beginning wrote many of the grants. Soon Jenny, Peter, and John, the artistic directors, took that over. We met interesting people in the city through the theatre company, and friends from Scarsdale came to see the shows.

In September 1992, I wrote a letter to the teachers, principals, and school superintendents in New York State about *A New Compact for Learning*. After welcoming everyone back to school, the letter continued:

> Let me begin by telling you where I think we are, as we begin the new school year. We continue to have some of the best schools and best students in the nation. We can be proud of what we achieved in the past, and confident that we will meet the needs of the future. There is no reason to bypass or give up on our public school system, as some of our critics seem ready to do today.
>
> At the same time, dramatic changes on the world scene and in our own country have increased the demands upon us exponentially. The well-being of our society depends directly on our success in educating each and all of our children to new high levels. We can't scale these heights just by working harder. We must make fundamental changes in the way we help our children learn. We have a game plan for making these changes with *A New Compact for Learning* approved by the Board of Regents in March 1991.
>
> The *Compact* is not a blueprint for change, but more like a traveler's guide for those who wish to make the journey. It sets forth basic principles, identifies the key players and the ways they should collaborate, and lists things the state will do to help local schools and school districts make the needed grass-root changes. Perhaps, most importantly, the

Compact will detail how we will provide top-down support for bottom-up reform.

Without question, the recession has hurt us in the past two years. It's hard to focus on the future when you're scrambling to survive. Nevertheless, since the *Compact* signing ceremony last September, we have made considerable progress in developing the infrastructure of support that will be needed as we pursue the *Compact*'s goals.

Through our curriculum and assessment council and our committees we are spelling out desired learning outcomes, what students should know and be able to do, and forming a new user-friendly program of assessment. We will distribute fact material for review and comment later this fall.

In the past, the state was vague about its curriculum requirements. The state required that students have three years of high school mathematics. But nowhere did the requirement define the skill or knowledge that was characterized by three years of mathematics. The three years could be three years of remedial arithmetic, or it could be a year each of intermediate algebra, solid geometry and calculus. It didn't matter. What "three years" meant was whatever anybody made it. We had a back door way of assessing what students took through the Regents Examination, but on average, in rough numbers, only about half the kids in the state took the exams.

What was clear was that there weren't any operative standards at all for the other half of the students. Our next step was to convene committees of teachers, people from the business community and other professions, and other involved laypersons to help us determine what students should come to know, and be able to do by the time they had finished each grade level.

This process was happening all over the country. I served as both a member and then chair of a national undertaking called the New Standards Project, which provided much of the intellectual firepower for the various reform movements going on state by state. I used to ask groups, "Tell me what English 9 is. How do you know when English 9 is over? You know how you know when English 9 is over?"

"When it's June," they would say, correctly.

"Exactly right. And you know what English kids take the next fall?"

"English 10," the audiences would respond.

I got to know the state very well during those years. I hadn't really known New York State before that. I didn't quite have that provincial attitude of *The New Yorker* cover cartoon that shows Fifth Avenue up to Tenth Avenue followed by Kansas, followed by Tokyo, but I certainly didn't appreciate the size and diversity of the state. The commissionership taught me quite a lot about that.

We adopted new regulations requiring districts to develop plans for participation by parents and teachers in school decision-making. In some districts, parents and teachers were already involved. However, in a great many, they were not. The process we were working toward is now called "shared decision-making." Students learn better when the home and the school work together. We created a structure in which people have to sit down and talk with one another about how the students' education is progressing. It was a difficult task to enact these regulations for a state as large and diverse as ours. Local teachers' unions and parent organizations differ from one another, and they often compete with each other. But eventually we did it. In some districts these parent/teacher committees are still functioning, a testament to their efficacy.

In recent decades, national organizations like the NCTM (National Council of Teachers of Mathematics) and the NCTE (National Council of Teachers of English) worked hard to develop similar curriculum standards. Many of the states would adopt these standards for use in their schools. Although there are variations from state to state, the essence is the same. The problem is that, although there is general agreement about curriculum standards (what ought to be taught), there is not much agreement on performance standards (how well students must do to show that they have mastered the content).

The disagreement on performance is as much a political issue as an educational one. In 2008, we saw the increase in student scores on Regents Examinations touted by Mayor Bloomberg during his reelection campaign. But these scores were later invalidated.

It's important to remember that the essence of the *Compact* was that the state would be clearer and more specific about what should be taught and learned, and that local school districts would have more autonomy in deciding how to realize those goals. The next step was to get teachers and parents more involved in school decision-making, as we have seen.

Thirdly, in order to make the *Compact* work, the State Education Department had to change as well. We began a major reorganization to get people out from behind the desks and into the field. Our goal was to become partners with field practitioners helping children to learn. That didn't work well at all. The people in the State Education Department resisted tooth and nail.

These bureaucrats weren't my bureaucrats. They were there when I arrived, and they knew they'd be there when I left. Ironically, the teachers, principals, and superintendents out in the field, many who had perennially railed against the rigid, narrow-minded bureaucrats from Albany, also fought this new initiative. They didn't want the state to get more involved in local operations.

The old style of operation for the State Education Department was to send inspectors out into the field to kick ass and take names. The new style, the one we were trying to cultivate, was to work in partnership with local people to nurture and develop their schools. It became clear after some six months of trying to make things happen that we weren't going to get anywhere within the traditional organization.

I drew together a few sympathetic souls from different parts of the department and organized them into a "Compact Action Team." They were to go out into the field, help school districts create "Compact Committees" and offer other technical help with the *Compact*. They accomplished a lot, but they also ended up alienating other members of the department.

The *Compact* called upon the state to be specific about what needed to be learned, but deliberately left a great deal of freedom to the schools and districts about how such learning could be achieved. Consequently, we had to get some of the department's procedural rules and regulations out of the way. We started to knock down regulatory tape that was in the way and encouraged people to try new ways of doing things.

Again and again I told practitioners that the form of schooling that we'd inherited over the last 150 years had become increasingly obsolete. None of us yet knew what the new form, or forms, of teaching should look like, but one thing was and remains certain: we needed a period of yeasty experimentation with new forms of organizing teaching and learning, new ways to think about schools and schooling. I encouraged that kind of experimentation insistently.

The idea was to identify schools that were successfully innovating and to connect them with other schools. All schools were to engage in a continuing appraisal of teaching and learning to best evaluate what works and what doesn't. To assist that ongoing process, we began to develop a program of school quality reviews, in which professional peers could provide both evaluation and support. Whenever I spoke to people, I emphasized that we could all learn a great deal from each other. That's when we began to recognize "Compact Partnership Schools." We conducted workshops where school practitioners could partner with each other to get ideas about what might work in similar situations.

I find it a plus that we got to know the state as well as we did. And our world was expanding beyond New York State as well. I was becoming known by the people in the world of education from my writings, from the press coverage, and from the interviews I gave on radio and television. We were invited to England to work with schools there. I gave speeches and spent time with educators at an institution with a wonderful name, "Her Majesty's Inspectorate." I learned about their school evaluation system.

The people from the Inspectorate later came to the United States offering wonderful opportunities to learn from them and to make new friends.

The program we developed was modeled after Her Majesty's Inspectorate. Instead of creating a new bureaucracy, we tapped practicing teachers and principals who were already in the schools and respected by their peers, to form teams and spend an entire week visiting a school and observing instruction. Afterward the team would meet with the school's staff and offer reflections and suggestions about what they had seen.

There are accrediting agencies that do something like this, but for the most part, those agencies do little other than produce written reports. This was to be a personal conversation, and hopefully more effective. Some school districts in the state are doing this ad hoc today.

In order to ensure smooth articulation between high school and college, our curriculum and assessment people worked closely with college faculty and administrators, especially at SUNY (the State University of New York). At the time, SUNY was developing standards for academic success in college. Our work was to ensure that these standards and high school graduation standards were consistent. We spent a lot of time with the SUNY people. They wanted to create standards for admission to college. We were revising our standards for graduation from high school. We wanted to make sure that the two meshed as closely as possible, so we had college faculty and high school teachers meeting with one another to work those things out, which they did to everyone's satisfaction.

The *Compact* also called for effective preparation for the work force. A task force sponsored by Lieutenant Governor Stan Lundine and co-chaired by Regent Walter Cooper and the New York State United Teachers President, Thomas Hobart, made important recommendations. Forums on these recommendations, cosponsored by the lieutenant governor and the Board of Regents, were conducted around the state. We worked with a national panel of experts in law and education finance in order to define what constituted adequate financial provisions for a sound basic education. We brought people from around the country together to work on it. We developed a set of indicators of progress by which we would measure our progress toward the goals of the *Compact*.

What did we accomplish with the *Compact*? First, we changed the state's relationship to local schools and school districts. We changed it from a top-down, hierarchical, you-guys-better-shape-up relationship, to one in which the state provides technical assistance to partners in a collaborative endeavor: top-down support for bottom-up reform.

Second, we reached out to businesses, community-based organizations, health and social service agencies, higher education, and other individuals and organizations to develop collaborative programs with the schools, bringing the strength of the entire community to bear on childhood education. This is the philosophy best summed up by the well-known Nigerian proverb, "It takes a village to raise a child," which Hillary Clinton used as the title for her 1996 book.

And third, we started the process of spelling out the standards by which we should teach and learn. Many parents and parent organizations praised the *Compact* for this reason: that at least it got them into the tent. In some tents things went well. But joint parent and teacher participation hasn't worked well everywhere. After Governor Pataki refused to fund the *Compact*, the State Education Department was unable to provide the kind of training people needed in order to make the most of that opportunity. Nevertheless there are many places where Compact Committees still exist and parents have access to and influence on their children's curricula.

In New York City, interestingly, the legislature picked up the idea of shared decision-making and enacted a law that requires what the regents had only created in regulation. All schools in New York City must have a planning team consisting of teachers, parents, and principals. It's a direct model on our 100.11 regulations.

If you look at the state as a whole, it's much harder to make a claim that the *Compact* made a huge difference. The bottom line for schools at the moment, is how well students do on tests or similar outcome measures. The historical record is that the dropout rate decreased during the period of time the *Compact* was being implemented, but I don't know whether it would have decreased if there hadn't been the *Compact*. We know that scores on tests of basic skills increased slightly, and that the gap between minority students and majority students decreased slightly, but I don't know whether the decrease occurred because of the *Compact* or whether it would have occurred anyway. Still, I'd rather accept credit than suffer blame. Let the record show that the *Compact* did no harm, and probably did some good. The *Compact* might have taken a greater foothold in the state's schools had Governor George Pataki not won the 1994 gubernatorial election and unseated Governor Mario Cuomo. Governor Pataki made drastic cuts in the funding for the State Education Department. Although the Board of Regents makes the state's educational policy, the governor and the legislature are responsible for the state budget. Without funding the Education Department cannot fulfill the regents' policy.

When Pataki took office and delivered his first budget message in January 1995, he said, "No more funding for *A New Compact for Learning.*" The press asked me about it, and I said I couldn't answer their questions because I hadn't had an opportunity to speak with the governor.

Instead I asked the reporters, "Which provision of the *Compact* does the governor object to? Is he opposed to clear and specific standards for student achievement? Is that his problem? Does he oppose the increased involvement of parents in their children's education? Is that the problem? Should we not be developing new assessments to measure student progress toward the goals that we have set? Is that his problem? Does he not wish to offer professional development to teachers so they can improve their skills and be better teachers for their students?"

One of the members of Governor Pataki's transition team, a woman who had worked for conservative think tanks in Florida, said that *A New Compact for Learning* was an attempt to "Africanize the curriculum." Her proof of that assertion apparently was that we quoted the Nigerian proverb, "It takes the whole village to raise a child." There were no objections to any of the actual initiatives we were undertaking.

If Governor Pataki had not been so hostile about my policies, particularly the *Compact*, I probably would have stayed in Albany for a few more years until it was a stable part of the system. I could have stayed. I had the votes. However, without funding and without caving in to the governor, the job might have been impossible. I am aware that changing New York's giant public school system, with all the social and economic issues that attend it, is probably not something that can be achieved in the course of one person's administration. Nevertheless, I will always wonder whether things would have been different if I had stayed longer.

During the '90s, education policy about teacher accountability was changing. Tests were becoming the gold standard of student assessment and teachers were being held accountable for poor student performance. "High-stakes" tests, used to make decisions about whether individual students would be promoted or retained, were being instituted in many states. By January of 1995, the future looked bleak.

During the 1994-1995 school year I began to think about retirement. I was sixty-five and not in the best physical condition. As I look back, I think of three events that influenced my decision.

The first was my annual evaluation by the regents, the previous June. Each year since I had become commissioner, the regents had conducted my evaluation through a process we had created together. The evaluation process had worked well, I felt. But in 1994 the regents decided to hire an outside consultant. In my opinion, the process went awry and was an unsatisfactory experience.

The second event was surgery on my spinal cord in October of 1994. Dr. Bennett Stein, chief of neurosurgery at the Neurological Institute in Manhattan, had discovered a thickening in my spinal cord. He thought the bulge might be a tumor and suggested surgery. The good news was there was no tumor; the bad news was that I had a vascular malformation in my spinal cord. There was no cure and no treatment. Eventually, I would lose the use of my legs and be confined to a wheelchair.

The third and decisive event was the election of Governor George Pataki. During the gubernatorial campaign, Pataki had made it clear he didn't support my agenda and would not fund it. A healthy majority of the regents supported both my agenda and me, and I probably could have stayed and fought Pataki. Harriet believed I should stay to see the *Compact* through. In retrospect I think she was right, but the idea of a protracted political fight, combined with my worsening physical condition and the bad taste the new evaluation process had left in my mouth all weighed heavily, and I decided I had had enough.

After Governor Pataki's inauguration he made a public issue of the residence. It was outrageous, he maintained, that the commissioner lived in such luxury at public expense.

If you remember, the Governor does not appoint the commissioner of education. The Board of Regents makes the appointment. But when Pataki took office, he convened his first cabinet meeting, and somebody sent me an invitation to a social event. I'm sure it was an error. However, I took some pains working behind the scenes to figure out whether or not I should attend. If I was invited and didn't show up, it would be insulting. On the other hand, if I showed up and was unexpected, that would be an embarrassment. I didn't know anyone in his organization who I could comfortably question, so I had to go through a third party. Finally, word filtered back to me that, since I got the damn invitation I had probably better show up whether he meant it or not, and play it by ear.

So I did, and I must say he and his wife Libby were friendly. The occasion was a dinner they were hosting in the Governor's Mansion in Albany. It was a lovely evening right after Christmas, and the governor was gracious to everybody there, including me. When we were having dessert, he had everybody stand up and say who they were. Almost everyone would say, "I'm Joe Blow, I'm the Secretary of Whatever, and I can't tell you how happy I am to be here. This is one of the best nights of my life." They all made that same kind of speech. I wasn't the last one to speak, but I was near the end.

I said, "Well, as most of you know, my name is Tom Sobol, and I am the skunk at this garden party. But I really want to express my thanks to the Governor and Mrs. Pataki for their gracious treatment this evening, because as somebody who doesn't really fit in with the rest of you, as we all know, I've been made to feel very comfortable and you all have been very friendly to me." I continued, "In fact, I feel so good about what's happened tonight, that I would like to invite you all to my place for dinner, but I can't because the Governor's selling it." I got a big hand for that, and a lot of warm laughter.

When I told the regents I intended to resign as of June 30, I didn't have a clue what I was going to do next. I knew I wanted to continue to work, but I didn't know what I was going to do. I had never left a job without having another one lined up. Not long after the news I was leaving became public, I received a call from Arthur Levine, the President of Teachers College at Columbia University.

He said, "Why don't you come on down here and work with us?"
I said, "To do what?"
He said, "I don't know. We'll think of something."

I was elated. Teachers College is one of the best graduate schools of education in the country. It is where I earned my doctorate, and I had often dreamed of teaching there.

Meanwhile, I had six more months as commissioner, and much work to get done. A group of New York City high schools was developing a new way of evaluating student progress. Instead of traditional testing, students would prepare portfolios of their written work, oral presentations, and other performance assessments. These would be critiqued by an assessment review panel consisting of the students, teachers, and members of the community, including college professors, business people, and lawyers. The plan would bypass the traditional Regents Examinations, with their heavy reliance on multiple-choice standardized testing.

Determined to continue its program, the Performance Assessment Committee asked me to waive the Regents Exam requirements for a five-year period, starting at once. There were good arguments, both political and pedagogical, for granting the waiver. I granted it with certain conditions, such as ongoing evaluations by the school districts and the State Education Department, on the grounds that you shouldn't invite people to do the very thing you won't let them do. I received the request for a waiver in early April 1995, when my time in office was running out—I had said in January that I would be leaving in June—and I was trying to gather up the loose ends and finish all my unfinished business. I knew that if we followed standard operating procedures it would be well into the fall before a decision was reached. So I wrote the decision myself and put it in the mail, bypassing dozens of staff members who normally participate in the decision-making process. Many of them are still outraged. But members of the Performance Assessment Committee, for whom I have the greatest respect, have given new meaning to high school graduation and improved the education of thousands of students.

The principle of equal educational opportunity is a cornerstone of our American democracy. All children, regardless of class, race, or religion are entitled to the resources and experiences needed for full participation in our society.

When did I first hear the phrase "equal educational opportunity?" It seems to be rooted in my grammar school past. Was it Miss Clausmeier? Miss Hartnett? Miss Lynch? Whichever of the three, she drummed home a cherished ideal. Unfortunately in many situations, particularly those involving children who live in poverty, the sad truth is that the most needy get the least help. Still, it is a worthy goal. It has motivated many students who regard it as part of their birthright.

The issue has been tried in the courts. In our constitutional scheme, education is a responsibility of the states, not the federal government. For over forty years, in over half the states, reformers have sought justice by bringing lawsuits arguing that the states were failing to meet this obligation under their respective state constitutions. They have had some important successes, but a general problem of inequality persists. The record shows such deep adherence to an unfair system that one can only conclude the majority of people want it to remain unfair.

In 1982, in *Levittown Union Free School District v. Nyquist*, the plaintiffs sought equal funding for schools and were dismissed by the New York Court of Appeals. The New York state constitution makes no provision for equal funding. In 1993 a new not-for-profit organization, the Campaign for Fiscal Equity (CFE), argued, in *CFE v. State*, that the funding for New York City school children was inadequate. Michael Rebell, aided by pro bono attorneys from a top New York City law firm, presented sufficient evidence to show that students were not receiving the sound, basic education the New York state constitution requires, and that these results were linked to inadequate funds. After nearly two decades of back-and-forth litigation, the court ruled in favor of CFE. The words of Chief Justice Leland DeGrasse are worth noting: "Demography is not destiny. The amount of melanin in a student's skin, the home country of her antecedents, the amount of money in the family bank account are not the inexorable determinants of academic success. All children are capable of seizing the opportunity of a sound basic education if they are given sufficient resources."

My role in this litigation was small, but zealous. Although I probably didn't think about it at the time, I am convinced that my desire to participate in this case was influenced by the years I had spent as a student in the public schools. I was a poor boy who had been good at school. All children, rich and poor, deserve a good education, and I wanted to be part of the good fight.

I took advantage of my position as commissioner to advocate for CFE's case. I talked to the legislature, teachers' unions, the School Boards Association, and almost anyone who would listen. Imagine my surprise when I looked at the cover page of the plaintiff's brief in the CFE case and saw on the list of named defendants (the governor and legislative leaders) that of "Thomas Sobol, Commissioner of Education." How could I defend the state's position when I had spent so much time attacking it? How could I get myself realigned so as to be among the plaintiffs?

I sought the advice of counsel from the State Education Department and the state attorney general. I couldn't be made a plaintiff, but I could drop out of the defense and become an amicus curia (an advisor to the court). That way I would not participate in argument but would be available to answer questions. This change of role had little or no impact on the trial. But I felt better and it set a precedent that others may consider.

It took a number of years for the case to come to trial. The court ruling that allowed the case to be tried was decided on June 13, 1995, just after I left the commissionership.

Harriet and I went home to Scarsdale with a great sense of relief at the end of June. In the years that have passed, neither Harriet nor I have said that we miss the residence, our life in Albany, or that we think of those times as part of "the good old days." What we do say is: wasn't it funny when so-and-so did *X*? Or: wasn't it great being with the kids when they did their summer Shakespeare thing? Or: How is Dave Johnson doing lately? How is Carole Huxley getting along? How are Kate and Bridget doing? We talk about individual people and we remember fond experiences, but we don't covet the life any longer. It was a good thing to have done, and I'm happy that it's now behind us.

As I come close to the end of this book, particularly the part covering my time as commissioner, I think of all that I would have missed had I not said yes to Chancellor Barell that March day in 1987 when he asked if I wanted the job.

Had I not been commissioner, I wouldn't have heard the Iroquois creation prayer from Lloyd Elm making our dining room feel holy in an ancient way. We would not have been the only people beside the three chiefs sitting in front of us at Governor Pataki's inauguration who didn't stand up and clap when the new governor promised to put capital punishment back in place in New York State. It was an unbelievable experience for us to spend time with Native American people, to be exposed to their way of looking at life and have the opportunity to appreciate the way they "walk in two cultures." I learned about the aura some people have, the palpable energy that radiates from their body, from a lawyer in the Iroquois tribe who served as a minority intern in the department and then returned to the reservation to work with her people.

I would not have spent as much time as I did with people of color, as we came to call them in those years: people who were black, Hispanic, or Asian. And it is not just the leaders I appreciated getting to know: president of the NAACP Hazel Dukes, Assemblyman Serrano, or Congressman Major Owens. I met people with their boots on the ground: parents who were serving as activists in the public school district, teachers working in the inner city, and children whose art hung in the residence.

Had I not been commissioner, we would have missed many celebrity events. One night Harriet and I were at a dinner hosted by the United Nations. Harriet sat next to a lovely woman who looked familiar. After dinner the woman stood up to speak. She turned out to be Audrey Hepburn, who was involved with UNICEF. We met college presidents, lobbyists, activists, Governor Mario Cuomo, legislative leaders, the Washington Delegation, and the late Senator Moynihan. Three or four times a year I went to Washington to lobby on the Hill. The trip almost always included an hour-long lecture by Senator Moynihan. You didn't talk with him. You listened. He was highly intelligent, well-informed, and entertaining, but I never got to say much.

The glitzy parts of that job were sometimes fun, sometimes a pain in the neck, and always time-consuming. There was too much real work to be done. The glitzy parts were not unreal, exactly, but they create their own reality. World figures live in the real world, and real things were happening. I'm not suggesting otherwise. But neither Harriet nor I felt we were permanent fixtures there. It was something we were only part of for a while.

Once, at a public event in East Harlem, the newly-appointed Federal Secretary of Education had just had his head handed to him by an irate parent who was unhappy with a school the secretary was advocating for. I was seated next to Bobby Wagner Jr., the former mayor of New York. The two of us grinned as jeers and catcalls rang throughout the crowded, hostile auditorium. "Welcome to New York, Mr. Secretary!" said Bobby, to no one in particular. Then, turning to me, he said, "Don't you love it! Isn't it great to be part of it?"

"I do love it, and it is great," I replied. "But Bobby, you have to understand that when this is over, I'll go home and paint the house, and I'll work in the garden out in the back, and I'll see my kids when I'm lucky. That's what I'll do. But you, you'll still be Bobby Wagner, and you'll be on the front page whenever you want. And you know what, that's okay with me."

He said, "I guess you're right."

I don't put it down at all, being at the center of things. But it always seemed impermanent to me, not based on genuine interpersonal relationships. It's not that it precluded such relationships, but being successful in that world involved knowing your place, who you knew, and who your connections were. After I left, people would ask, "Do you miss the power?" I don't miss the opulent residence and I don't miss associating with people whose photographs get in the paper all the time. The value of power for me was being in a position where I could make good things happen. I miss that.

CHAPTER 7

Teachers College, Columbia University

My first days at Columbia were strange. I felt as if I had died. I went abruptly from my Albany office, which even in my waning weeks was a center of hyperkinetic activity (constantly ringing phones, people waiting in the hall) and where planned agendas were trumped by constant emergencies, to silence. In my Teachers College office there were no people, no ringing phones.

For a while, with the silence screaming at me, I just sat there. Eventually, gathering all my strength, I put the books up on the bookshelves. The phone didn't ring. There were no meetings to go to, and nobody was around. So I looked at the books for a while, and then I rearranged them.

All my life I have been surrounded by smart women who have made me look good by doing my paperwork and keeping me organized. But on that first day, I was alone. I recall taking my yellow pad and my No. 2 pencil and scribbling out a memorandum to someone, then putting it in the outbox, where I expected someone would take it, type it, and mail it for me. However, when I came back the next day, it was still there. I realized I had better learn to use the computer.

But my role at Teachers College quickly began to expand. I was appointed to fill a newly established chair entitled the Christian A. Johnson Professor of Outstanding Educational Practice. I was a lone-wolf practitioner among the academic sharks on the faculty. I served in the position until I retired in 2007, when I assumed emeritus status and taught part-time for two more years. What did I do during all that time?

Primarily, I taught. Linda Darling-Hammond, whom I had invited to be a consultant to the Board of Regents and for whom I have the utmost respect, was leaving to accept a position at Stanford University. She kindly gave me a copy of her description for a course called Curriculum and Teaching Policy. I took it, modified it to reflect the recent literature in the field, and taught it each year for the next fifteen years, making it increasingly mine as time passed by. (The course was like Grandpa's axe, which despite having five new heads and six new handles over the years was still considered the same old axe, still hanging on the same old hook down in the cellar.)

I also developed and taught a course called Ethical Issues in Educational Leadership, in which aspiring leaders explored the ethical dimensions of conflicts in their lives and work situations. The course was an immediate hit and remained popular throughout my years at the college. These two courses formed the spine of my teaching activity.

Over the years, however, I taught other courses on various aspects of educational leadership. Together with my colleague Dr. Gibran Majdalany I reorganized and conducted the Inquiry Program, a doctoral program designed to prepare aspiring school superintendents and other leaders. I planned and ran the Superintendents Work Conference, an annual July event for forty to fifty public school superintendents representing urban, suburban, and rural school districts. Since its origin in the 1940s, the conference has provided an opportunity for participants to meet with some of the nation's leaders in education. We had superintendents from New York City, San Francisco, Dallas, and Detroit, but also medium-sized cities like

Richmond, Omaha, Tallahassee, and San Diego as well as from suburbs and rural areas. Each year we created a theme and invited well-known people in education and other fields to speak. Afterward we would divide up into small groups for discussion. The variety of experience of the attendees was an excellent stimulus for discussion.

Part of the fun of the experience was getting people who would be unlikely to ever meet or speak sit down and compare notes about their respective problems. One summer we had a big blond man from a small district in Minnesota and a black woman from District 26 in Queens. During the seminars, I noticed they both spoke out, often expressing conflicting opinions. That evening's social event was a cruise around Manhattan Island. They sat with one another over a beer and carried on a spirited debate while onlookers cheered them on. During the next year, I received emails from both of them telling me they were still in touch with each other. During that same cruise, Harriet and I sat next to a young superintendent from Iowa who had never been to New York before. As we passed the Statue of Liberty tears ran down his cheeks.

I conceived of, developed, ran, and taught in the Future School Administrators Academy, a shortcut to state certification for school administrators. Many of the districts in Westchester and Putnam Counties had expressed a need for talented principals. With the cooperation of Renee Gargano, the Assistant Superintendent of the Northern BOCES (Board of Cooperative Services), Teachers College, and the Department of Education in Albany, I arranged for certification from the state. Many of the leaders in the area were trained in the FSAA, satisfying the need for certified administrators in Putnam and Westchester. For eight years, every Thursday, I taught classes to talented teachers looking for career advancement, who were recommended by their supervisors.

In addition, I engaged in the following activities:
- I advised about one hundred or more individual doctoral students,

sponsoring their doctoral dissertations and guiding them in their professional and personal lives.

- I maintained a full calendar of speaking engagements, both locally and nationally.
- I served on the governing boards of the Council of Chief State School Officers and the New Standards project, among others.
- I testified as an expert witness in school finance lawsuits in New York and California.
- Finally, in my spare time I played the role of the elder statesman.

The role and the situation were a natural for me. I was old enough to know both a little about a lot and a lot about a little, but I didn't have enough power to threaten anyone. For the first time in many moons I wasn't running the place I worked in. I couldn't cut someone's budget or fire anyone. I was safe. People could talk to me. And did they ever!

For the first ten years, I made it my business to be in my office every workday (and many Saturdays) from mid-morning, when New York City's morning traffic rush was over, until after the evening rush.

By the time I testified in the CFE trial, I had been at Teachers College for a number of years. Getting up the stairs into the Court of Appeals in lower Manhattan was the most difficult part of the experience. My colleague Gibran helped me as he always did when I had to go places. I had been using forearm canes for a couple of years but had recently begun using an electric scooter for longer distances. Fortunately, there was an elevator inside to the courtroom. Some of the trial was fun. The attorneys were arguing about whether class size impacted the quality of education. The judge looked to me and asked if I had an opinion on either side of the question. I said no, but added that I had never heard a parent complain that his or her child's class was too small. The judge incorporated my remark into his decision.

One day of the trial was particularly memorable to me. I was giving testimony. A class from a local junior high school had come to observe the proceedings. The students arrived just as I was opening the door to enter the courthouse. I turned to face them. They stood on the steps below me, their teacher behind them.

"I'm a little nervous today because I'll be testifying. Can you help me out?" I asked them.

"How?" they asked, looking puzzled.

"Smile and give me a thumbs-up if you think I've made a good point. If you do that, I'd feel really good." All of them smiled and some of them practiced their thumbs-up. That was a good day for me. During my testimony, when I made a particular point, they all smiled and slowly did a quiet thumbs-up.

As the CFE case progressed through the courts, it became necessary to define the "sound basic education" to which each student is entitled. One justice at the appellate level expressed the view that a sound basic education was a middle school education. His view was hooted down. Others proposed a high school education. But what does that entail? In many high schools, even today, the courses are what each teacher makes of them. Several others proffered elegant statements that the court dismissed as aspirational. It was clear that the state needed standards that specified what students should know and be able to do, subject by subject, year by year.

Fortunately, such a system of standards and assessments was already in development. At the direction of the Board of Regents and the commissioner, and with the help of teachers in schools and colleges throughout the state, the State Education Department had been designing rubrics and tests and setting performance standards that students would be expected to meet.

I had initiated a standards program for New York , and I clearly remember the day when, as I finished writing my recommendation to the regents, I said to myself, "Whatever else, this standards program should help with our finance litigation." It did.

Teachers College cares about people with disabling conditions. With so many students taking courses in psychology and special education, it takes special care of faculty members who are themselves disabled. To this end it had designated the six-car parking lot next to the Main Hall and in front of the E. K. Thorndike building (named for a distinguished psychologist) as parking for disabled faculty only. As someone who walked with two fore-arm canes and drove a car outfitted with hand controls, I was an eligible user of the parking lot. Here's how it worked.

The lot lies between two buildings at the end of a short alley with a locked iron gate. To get in, I would have to drive my Volvo off the street, across the sidewalk and into an alley, stopping before I reached the gate. I would get out of the car, maintaining my balance by holding a grab-bar affixed to the car door frame, and reach back inside to get my canes on the passenger's side floor. Using the canes, I would hobble up, then lean the canes against the gate and reach into my pants pocket to get the padlock key. The gate was made of heavy, one-inch-round iron spikes welded to-gether, approximately four feet high and twelve feet wide. It was unlocked by maneuvering a super heavy spike up from a snugly-fit iron receptacle buried in the ground. Thus I would need to find the key, open the lock, jiggle the spike, and push the gate open. I could then get back into the car (no easy task) and drive through the gateway along in the alley, whereupon I would have to stop and get back out of the car, hobble back and lock the gate. Having locked the gate, I could finally get back to my car and find a parking space. I may have forgotten a step or two. Even so, what a classical Catch-22: if you can deal with the padlocked gate in the alley, you prob-ably don't need a parking space!

Fortunately, by the time I began using an electric wheelchair, the gate was replaced by a guard stationed inside a booth. Conditions inside the building were much more friendly. I shared an office suite with Gibran and my competent assistant Gosia Kolb. There was one office for him, one office for me, and an outer office for Gosia. We announced an open-door policy. We furnished the rooms with a coffee pot, a cookie jar, and a plentiful stash of pistachio nuts and awaited a response. We didn't have to wait long. The students began visiting in droves.

Gibran and his wife, also named Gosia, brought an added dimension to my personal and professional life. Gibran said many times, "I am your brother. If necessary, I will carry you on my shoulders." He is a stocky Lebanese man, always dressed well, about twenty-five years younger than I am. He exudes warmth. There were times he almost did carry me on his shoulders. When I could no longer use my van's hand controls, he would drive to my house, park his car, and drive me to Teachers College in the van. On the reverse trip he never left my home until I was safely in the house.

Gibran had been at Teachers College long before I arrived. He was born in Lebanon to an intellectual Christian family, and had immigrated to the United States to attend college. After college, he earned his doctorate at Teachers College and then remained, helping to run the annual Superintendent's Conference. In many ways, he was the chief of staff of the conference. Superintendents and students loved him. Harriet and I love both him and his wife.

We became family when he married Gosia. Gosia was a young Polish woman who was in Scarsdale helping a relative of hers (evidently Gosia is a common Polish nickname). Scarsdale is not filled with young unmarried Polish women, or many unmarried women at all for that matter. The town is filled with families, and Gosia felt lonely and isolated. One spring, she registered for Harriet's writing group. The group fell in love with her. She and Harriet became friends. We invited her to help us out at the Superintendent's Conference so that she might meet some students her age.

To our surprise she and Gibran spent the conference together. Six months later, they were married. We hosted a great party for them, and Harriet added them to our seder list.

Gibran, Gosia Kolb, and I were in our offices five days a week. Our doors were always open. When students dropped in we talked to them about their studies, but we also asked how their lives were going. I have the utmost respect for the students at Teachers College. They are diverse in every significant respect: race, color, creed, religion, nationality, socioeconomic status, and sexual orientation. They take their studies seriously and they're good at them. And most of the students truly believe that if they work hard enough and hold true to their values they can make the world a better place.

Sometimes the professional spilled over into the personal, as it did with Gibran, his wife Gosia, and Gosia Kolb. We threw a party for Gibran and his wife Gosia after their wedding. Gibran and the two Gosias came to dinner at our home. We went to their homes. One of my students, Gina Chen, also became a personal friend. Gina is an attractive young woman from a traditional Chinese-American family in Los Angeles. She was younger than most of our students, having come to our master's degree program directly from college. The combination of her youth, her family background, the electricity of New York City, and the fact that she had no prior experience teaching made her entry into the master's program a difficult transition. She needed a place to anchor her ship, and happily she chose our office. She became one of our staunch office groupies, dropping in to chat two or three times a week, in addition to taking one of my courses each semester. We had serious conversations and laughing spells, as the academic year ground on in its inexorable way.

In the spring Gina completed her program and went back to Los Angeles. At Christmas she sent me a card, and I replied. The following year we exchanged Christmas cards again. Then, one August afternoon, the telephone rang. It was Gina!

"Dr. Sobol?" she asked.

"Gina!" I said. "How are you? It's so good to hear from you!"

She told me she was fine. I told her I was fine as well. Then, in an effort to get to the purpose of the call, I asked, "So, Gina, what's up? What can I do for you?"

"I have something special to ask you," she replied. "Will you marry me?"

For a long moment I was speechless as my mind raced through possible responses, such as, "Gina, of course I'll marry you...I have two or three things to take care of...but hey! No problem!" Fortunately my better self took hold. I realized that she was asking me to officiate her wedding, and I bumbled out something like, "How nice of you! Let's talk about it!"

And so we began a splendid adventure. I won't weary you with all the details, but here are the major steps along the way:

- Gina and I engaged in serious cross-continental conversations about her life and her fiancé Dat.
- I learned that Dat was Vietnamese, one of the "boat people" who set to sea and sought safe harbor when the war was ending.
- I learned that after many rebuffs Dat and his family managed to board one of the last ships leaving Vietnam. A Catholic church in Seattle had sponsored him and his mother. The church got them settled and helped in their adjustment to the United States.
- I learned that Gina's parents at first opposed her marrying a Roman Catholic man but eventually relented when Gina persisted.
- I learned that I was asked to officiate at the wedding service because I was old enough, safe enough, and religiously neutral enough to be tepidly acceptable to all parties.

My only qualm, as I told Gina, was that I had no legal authority to perform her wedding ceremony. Gina explained that I could register as an ordained minister with the Universal Life Church, which under California law would grant me the authority to perform wedding ceremonies (the ULC has been ordaining any and every person who wants to be a minister, for free, since 1959. Nowadays it takes about 30 seconds through their website).

Harriet and I had breakfast with Gina and Dat twice in California to discuss their life together and plan the wedding ceremony. On a beautiful afternoon in late spring, outdoors in somebody's magnificent private garden, I was honored to lead the ceremony at Gina's wedding.

Gina was among the many students who were surprised to find that at Teachers College teaching took second place to faculty research.

The tension between theory and practice poses questions for many graduate schools in medicine, law, business, social work, and architecture as well as in education. What should be the ratio between these two fundamental variables? Should it be a fifty-fifty balance, or should one side of the equation be given more emphasis than the other? What approach is most likely to produce the highly qualified professionals our students wish to become?

At Teachers College, the department to which I was assigned (Organization and Leadership), emphasized theory and minimized practice. Many of the professors believe that theory is hydraulics, whereas practice is plumbing. Did I want to make plumbers?

Lacing up my practitioner's gloves, I slugged it out in a series of memos with two tenured faculty members. "You need both," I said. "Theory without practice is ungrounded abstraction. Practice without theory is one event after another without pattern or meaning. Do you understand?"

They did not agree.

The faculty took great care to prevent practitioners from corrupting the academic environment. Adjunct faculty (typically, superintendents or other leaders from the field of practice) were hired only occasionally and were not eligible for tenure. They could not serve longer than five years. They had little voice in matters of governance. And, along with the regular faculty, they could be penalized for spending too much time with students. Imagine, at Teachers College, the presumed citadel of teaching and learning, subordinating students' eagerness to learn to professors' eagerness to publish!

One talented young professor was refused tenure for spending too much time with TC students in the schools. She hadn't published enough to be granted tenure was the tenure committee's decision. The experience she had gained helping TC students learn how to be in the classroom didn't have the value that publishing did, the committee decided.

She was as they say "boots on the ground," helping TC students become teachers. She was doing what she should be doing and she had valuable information about practice to bring to the TC table, but she hadn't published enough. In the end, she took her experience to another college where she became a valuable member of the faculty.

At Teachers College I was virtually a lone practitioner in a sea of academics, all socialized in the same culture and convinced that their view of the world is the only intellectually respectable view to hold. It seemed like a curious view sometimes. It holds, for example, that knowledge derived from the basic social sciences (psychology, sociology, economics), is refined through the applied sciences (management science, organizational behavior), and is then acted upon by practitioners. The job of the academy, therefore, is to teach theory. And the job of the students is to apply it. The notion that knowledge might be gained from practice or that there are ways of knowing not based in theory is regarded as dim-witted and barbaric. Another of the academy's curious views is that no knowledge exists until the academy itself creates it. Superintendents and principals and teachers can find better ways to meet kids' needs. They can generate ideas, create programs, secure the necessary staff and community support, fight off the wolves on the board and in the press, and even evaluate what they have done and make improvements. But they do not know anything until an academic comes along, writes up what the practitioners are doing, publishes an article read only by other academics, and then takes credit for having "created" new knowledge. Small wonder that I spent much of my time in good-natured debate with most of my colleagues.

My point is that theory and practice should be inextricably bound together. If theory exists in a vacuum, in the academy, what good does it do for children? Academics and students should be in the schools in the way that professors of medicine and their students are in the hospital together. Practitioners' experience should be welcome in the academy. One needs the other. One learns from the other. Students would benefit from the academics' and practitioners' joint venture.

Am I complaining too much? Have I become an old crank, no longer able to appreciate the life of the professorial mind? I don't think so. I maintain that you need both teaching and publishing, just as you need both theory and practice. I simply want to reverse the order of priority. Students first!

Teachers College was founded to educate teachers for the schools of New York City. It should return to that historic mission. With teaching and learning as its central purpose, not only would the city be better served, the nation would be reminded how rich and life-shaping an education can be when it is provided by teachers who have mastered their profession, and who place students first. Think John Dewey.

That having been said, I enjoyed my years at Teachers College. The students were wonderful and my sort-of colleagues occasionally connected with their students and reached new heights (Morningside). By 2005, my physical condition had deteriorated to the point that I was using an electric wheelchair. The malformation in the capillaries of my spinal cord had done their job. I had also been diagnosed with Parkinson's disease. I continued to love my students and my teaching but every day was an effort.

Teachers College gave me a medal some time ago, for distinguished service, I believe. I don't know what "distinguished service" means, but I thanked them for the honor. I am happy for the many honors I've received. One needs them to offset the bad times. But my satisfaction is deeper, more pervasive, more quiet and enduring. True satisfaction is not found in being recognized for doing work, it is found in doing the work. I love what I do, and I have been fortunate to have places to do it in. Every day was a source of satisfaction.

Ethical Issues in Educational Leadership

The following pages are drawn from an essay I wrote entitled, "The Principal As Moral Leader," which is contained in *The Principal Challenge*, edited by Marc Tucker and Judy Codding. The material in the essay is drawn from a course I created at Teachers College called Ethical Issues in Educational Leadership. I taught the class almost every year I was at the college. It always had a large enrollment. Often we had to cap it at forty students. I am proud of the course and the students who shared those sessions with me. I hope it answers the question, "How do teachers and administrators live their profession and lives ethically?"

The essay begins with a scenario I created for the class:

Juan Ruiz tilted back in his office chair and stared idly at the banner. *Somos Uno*, it said. That's a laugh, he thought. He remembered the day the kids had tacked it up: they were so proud and happy. Not just the banner but the whole world seemed to be coming down.

Juan was halfway through his second year as a junior high school principal. He had been surprised when he got the job, because he had no prior experience as a principal. But his superintendent, Tony Mercado, had stuck his neck out for him. "Juan is okay," he told the board. "He's great with kids and he's completely loyal."

Juan closed his eyes. That's another one, he thought.

Located in a run-down, violent, city neighborhood, the school had been a problem for years. Teachers put in their time and left early. Fights broke out often. Test scores were low. Juan had been, and still was, determined to turn it around. Intuitively, he knew he had to connect with the kids and make them feel that they counted for something. He also knew he had to find the teachers who hadn't given up and give them some tangible reason for hope. The first year, he spent a lot of time listening to people and finding small things to do to show both kids and teachers that he was paying attention. Slowly, the atmosphere began to change. Then, last September, they started the Somos Uno campaign, and even the burned-out teachers began to get enthusiastic about the place.

The campaign was a set of activities designed to bring people together and help them feel pride in themselves and their school. It included a multicultural festival for students and families, an "English-plus" approach to bilingual education, and community meetings to hash out school problems. Juan himself was surprised at how well it all worked. But the test scores didn't go up. In fact, the midyear eighth-grade reading and math scores, already low, declined a bit. The superintendent, whose job was on the line, had told Juan that he had to scrap the Somos Uno program in order to devote more time to test preparation. When word reached teachers and parents, they raised the roof. They told Juan that if he wanted their respect as a principal, he'd better defend their program against the superintendent and that ignorant Board of Education.

Juan had tried. In fact, he had just come back from Mercado's office. Mercado himself had seemed troubled, but in the end, he had said, "Juan, what do you want from me? You want me to tell my wife and kids that I'm out of here? Drop the program, and leave me alone."

Juan rubbed his eyes and looked at the banner once more. What should he do? Should he drop the program as ordered? Should he organize a community appeal to the Board of Education? Should he pretend to drop the program while actually continuing it? Should he ask for a transfer or look for another job?

Mostly, he wondered who deserved his loyalty more. Was it the superintendent who had hired him, the staff and parents, or the kids, whom he loved? Or was it his own parents, their silent voices telling him from beyond how proud they were of him and how they wanted him to be strong? What was his conception of personal and professional integrity? And was it fair to risk getting himself in trouble, given that it affected not only him, but also his wife? Didn't he owe loyalty to her?

All the forty-five graduate students in my class on Ethical Issues in Educational Leadership had read the scenario. It's about a quarter to nine on a Thursday night (the class meets between 7:10 and 9:00 p.m.), but neither the students nor I show signs of relaxation. The students have been meeting in groups of four or five to make up their minds and sharpen their arguments about the questions I had asked at the end of the scenario. Now, it's time to share their thinking with the class as a whole. I say little. The questions I raise are to clarify presentations or to suggest implications for further thought. After one presentation, I ask how many have experienced similar situations on their jobs. Half the students raise their hands. "I *am* Juan!" shouts a young man. The class laughs.

Later, I ask, "What would Nel Noddings do?" The students smile again; Noddings is one of their favorites, and the teacher's question has become a mantra. One year a class arrived wearing t-shirts with the letters WWNND (What Would Nel Noddings Do?) across their chests. Nel Noddings, a Stanford professor, believes that the relationship between teacher and student be a caring one. In a caring relationship, both the carer and the cared-for person benefit. The carer listens to what the cared-for person says and thinks about it. The carer's energy goes toward the cared-for person and hopefully helps that person. In Noddings's theory, the cared-for person must be aware of being cared-for. In this relationship both benefit, but in different ways.

Toward the end of the session students press me for my answers to the questions about Juan's situation. To their frustration, I refuse to do so. "Write about it in your logs," I say. "I'll see you next week."

Ethical Issues for Educational Leadership was a popular course before it ever met, and it became more popular as time passed. I suspect it filled a real need on the part of the students. I was delighted they felt that need because I have always believed that teachers, principals, etc., have a sacred trust when they interact with children. The class started with forty-odd students enrolled in the first course, eighty in the second. Thereafter, attendance was capped at forty. It was evident that the graduate students taking the course, chiefly future principals and superintendents, were eager to explore ways of thinking about the dozens of decisions they would make each day, decisions that are not determined by law or regulation but are still of the utmost importance to the individuals involved.

As a student once said, "We need more to go on than flying blind."

Students were required to read works by Aristotle, Immanuel Kant, Nel Noddings, Machiavelli, Joseph Badaracco, Michael Apple, William Bennett, Wendell Berry, John Goodlad, Martin Luther King Jr., Jonathan Kozol, Thomas Sergiovanni, Kenneth Strike, Mark Twain, Edward O. Wilson, Bongsoon Zubay, and others. The first three writers provide three fundamentally different perspectives from which to view the nature and origin of ethical systems. All of the reading was applied to case studies drawn from the literature and the students' real-world practice. As a rule of thumb, the first hour of each session was devoted to theory and the second to practice. Each session, however, took its own shape depending upon student interest.

Why Study Ethics?

Why should school leaders study ethics? The reasons for studying ethics lie in the nature of education, schools, and leadership. Education is an inherently moral matter. It is moral because people develop (or fail to develop) morally as well as physically, emotionally, and intellectually. It is moral because teaching—helping to shape other people's minds, sensibilities, and capabilities—raises deep questions of purpose, values, and responsibility. It is moral because it involves the relationship between one generation and another, a relationship that helps determine the direction and quality of human life.

Schools and schooling are inherently moral as well. Not only are they charged with the moral purpose of education, but as social institutions they constitute a rich soup of human relationships and interactions through which children learn a moral code. For most children, school is life, not just preparation for it. And children learn from the lives they lead, not just from their lessons. If we want our children to lead ethical lives, their schools and the adults in them should model ethical behavior.

We all know there are teachers who punish children for not writing neatly when the child has a learning disability. We know there are teachers who call their students "stupid." We know there are superintendents who don't support their librarians when the school board wants to censor a library book.

In this class, students kept logs. They recorded ethical issues in their working life and their own responses. The ethics lessons were lived. They were real.

Educational leadership raises the moral stakes. Educational leaders have the power and the duty to influence the education of a large number of students. Moreover, they work in organizations and complex political environments wherein competing values and beliefs must be moderated toward wise and just ends. Such enterprises cannot be conducted well by administrative technique or politics alone. They must be informed by a larger sense of purpose and guided by clearly delineated ethical considerations.

Furthermore, educational leaders have power, including information, positional authority, and control of resources. How they use that power is a profoundly moral matter. As Tom Sergiovanni has written:

> Whenever there is an unequal distribution of power between two people, the relationship becomes a moral one. Whether intended or not, leadership involves an offer to control. The follower accepts this offer on the assumption that control will not be exploited. In this sense, leadership is not a right but a responsibility.

There is yet another reason for paying attention to ethics. The moral nature of leadership is a largely unrecognized and untapped source of motivation for the education profession. Most of the people who become teachers or school administrators do so because they want to help children. The draw and the rewards are those endemic to the helping professions: a sense of moral purpose and commitment, being part of a larger cause, and doing good for others. Inevitably, as time passes, these original motives become partly buried beneath the baggage of other human needs: esteem, recognition, variety, power, and material success. But the core values and motives remain. And precisely because education cannot compete with Mammon on Mammon's terms, it is to this core that we must appeal if we want our education leaders to remain committed to their profession.

We must recognize the moral nature of the education enterprise, and honor those who see their work as a calling and act accordingly. Few people can be energized for a lifetime by the pursuit of higher test scores. Many are hungry for an opportunity to be part of a moral cause. Policy makers who advocate financial incentives for improved performance are off-target. Able teachers and administrators will take more money if it is offered, of course. They are not stupid. But what most good teachers really want is to make their lives meaningful by serving others. We need to learn how to tap into this deep well of human motivation.

Does the Public Want Ethical Schools?

America's public schools serve a vast and diverse constituency. People differ widely in their aspirations, attitudes, values, and sense of how things should be done and how people should behave. Given these realities, is it right for the public schools to impose a uniform ethical vision? Is there sufficient agreement among the public on ethical matters to justify preparing educational leaders to think and act ethically?

Such questions are not as difficult as they may at first seem. There is a core of civic values to which most people in our society subscribe. These include democracy, the rule of law, majority rule, and minority rights. Schools need not shrink from asserting such values. Similarly, there is a core of personal virtues most people prize, including honesty, integrity, responsibility for one's actions, and respect for property and for life. In general, these virtues are not in dispute. On broad and basic matters such as these, where most of the public is in full agreement, the public schools and their leaders have not only a right, but a duty to take a positive ethical stand.

The problem arises when one digs beneath that level of generality. What seems clearly right or wrong in the abstract may be difficult to unravel in particular circumstances. Indeed, part of the educational leader's job is to sort through the facts and figure out how general principles are best applied. When you get down to specific cases, reasonable people may differ, and an individual must use her or his own judgment.

Does the public want educational leaders to exercise such judgment? The question is moot. The fact is that principals, superintendents, and other leaders must make decisions with moral consequences all the time. There is no other way to operate a school. But whether or not leaders have the ethical training to make such decisions is paramount. In our democratic society, the role of the educational leader is not to impose a personal vision of morality on others. It is to act ethically in one's own terms and to foster a dialogue through which differing conceptions of ethics can be expressed and considered in the course of shaping a shared ethical vision. In our democratic society, the leader is not a high priest or a gospel preacher; he is a member of a community, teaching others and learning from others and shaping his own attitudes and behavior as well as those of others. Some writers describe the role as "servant-leader." If one understands the word servant in its most exalted meaning, that sounds right.

Of course, the public is divided on larger issues as well. Vast differences exist on such education-specific matters as vouchers, high-stakes testing, educational equity, and desegregation, not to mention social issues that impact schools, like abortion, sexual identity, race, socioeconomic status, or whether teachers should wear neckties. Whenever important matters are in dispute it seems wrong for public school officials to take a unilateral stand. Here again, the role of the leader is to foster and participate in a public dialogue, where all the issues may be debated vigorously. In the public system, ethics sometimes consists of maintaining the fairness and integrity of the democratic process.

All of these considerations argue for ethics being a part of schools and ethical training being necessary for school leaders. In the end, advocates of ethics in schools have history on their side. From the days of *The New England Primer* and McGuffey's *Readers* on down to the present, Americans have almost always wanted their schools to produce character as well as competence. Ask parents what they want for their children. Yes, they want their children to do well on tests, go to college, get good jobs. But almost universally, they also want them to become decent people and responsible citizens: i.e., to lead good lives. And they believe that the schools should play a role in helping them do so.

Do the Great Neck Village School and the Scarsdale Alternative School add to the ethical climate of the community? I would argue that they do, not only for the students but for the community at large. There is a ripple effect. The students take their moral education and share it with their parents, siblings, and friends. Parents tell other parents about what happened yesterday at a community meeting. Friends tell friends. School news in a community spreads like wildfire. "Did you hear about the A-School kid who was fresh to the superintendent? No, she wasn't suspended. She went up in front of the Fairness Committee."

What Does Being Ethical Mean?

As has been noted, there is no guidebook, no simple set of principles or rules to answer this question. In much of what they do, educational leaders must work hard to discover what the most ethical choice is in the specific situations that confront them. However, we know enough from the writing and experience of wise and thoughtful people who have preceded us to be able to describe the general landscape. Here are some of the features of that landscape, presented not from the lofty standpoint of a philosopher but from the perspective of an on-the-ground education practitioner.

Being ethical and acting ethically do not mean simply keeping your nose clean. The conventional view (and the gist of most codes of ethics) is that ethics means not doing wrong. Ethical leaders, in this view, should not lie, cheat, steal, goof off, or hurt people. That is good advice, as far as it goes. Leaders should not lie, cheat, steal, loaf, or hurt people.

But avoiding doing wrong is not enough. The moral imperative for educational leaders is to also do right. People who are entrusted with the education of children and young people have an affirmative duty of care. They are responsible for the education and welfare of the students in their charge, and this responsibility must be carried out through positive action. They must create an environment in which effective teaching and learning can flourish. They must develop and sustain wholesome and productive relationships with their students and their staff. They must draw on their knowledge and experience to guard their charges from harm and to create new opportunities for growth.

All of this requires proactive, sustained engagement with the life and activity around them. Carol Gilligan (1993) writes about the importance of "stepping in" as opposed to "stepping out." All people, but especially those charged with a duty of care, must "step in" to the confusion and messiness of human life, forging relationships with all kinds of others and making a positive contribution to their lives. Retreating to the office and staying out of trouble is not ethical. Making good things happen for people is.

Making good things happen for people is not always easy. It requires skill, knowledge, courage, and persistence. Leaders must be both ethical and competent. A leader who is pure of heart but ineffective on the job is not of much use. As Sergiovanni has said, "The challenge of leadership is to make peace with two competing imperatives, the managerial and the moral." Consequently, leaders have an obligation to develop their skills and expand their knowledge as fully as possible. Avoidable ignorance, where it affects children's education, is unethical.

So is incompetence. In his book, *Defining Moments*, Joseph Badaracco writes about virtue and virtu. According to Badaracco, "Virtu was Machiavelli's word for the moral code of public life. The word is not an antiquated version of virtue, for it means something quite different. Virtu is a combination of vigor, confidence, imagination, shrewdness, boldness, practical skills, personal force, determination, and self-discipline." To discharge their responsibilities ethically, educational leaders must have both qualities. Being good without being effective does not help much. Being effective without being good can be awful. The two must go together. As James O'Toole has written, "While morality is a necessary ingredient of leadership, it is not sufficient. The Rushmore Standard of Excellence is the twofold ability to lead change both morally and effectively."

Being ethical also means more than choosing right instead of wrong. As we have seen, in the complex world of schools, the choices that need to be made are often between right and right (or wrong and wrong—"the lesser of the two evils"). Being ethical in such cases means being alert to the ethical dimensions of a situation, reflecting on these ethical implications, and choosing as wisely as possible. It also means knowing when to bend and when to draw the line. Leaders cannot wage a to-the-death fight on every issue, even if they are in the right. (Don Quixote is an appealing figure, but he would be a disaster as a superintendent.) But neither should they sell out—"go along to get along." Perhaps this sounds like equivocation. It is not. It is real life. Being ethical means knowing when to take a stand and when not to. Sometimes it is easy; sometimes it is not. There is no absolute standard to guide you. But every ethical leader knows deep down what choice is called for in these defining moments, as Badaracco calls them.

Did I do the right thing when I let *A Curriculum of Inclusion* go public? The right thing for whom? It probably wasn't the right thing for me in my career, but it was a defining moment for me because it was right in a global sense. Sam Walton explained it to me when he said he never thought he would be sitting in the elegant commissioner's office helping to decide what the NYS social studies curriculum would be. Would I have released the report if I had known the abuse I would endure? I don't know. Was it the ethical thing to do? I thought it was the ethical thing to do then and I think so now.

Sometimes such defining moments can shape a leader's career. But there is more to being ethical than choosing wisely on the grand occasions. What also counts is who you are and how you act from day to day.

Education leaders interact with scores of other people daily, and the quality of those interactions becomes part of the fabric of school life. How does the leader relate to peers? To superiors? To students? To the rank and file of the staff? To the woman who answers the telephone, the man who sweeps the floor? Are these people valued for themselves, or do they merely serve some end? In Noddings's terms (1984), do they fall within the leader's circle of care? And then there is the leader's "own" work. How responsibly is it done? What standards of quality does the leader meet at those inevitable times when one is tired and no one is looking? We all get tired, and only the saints can do their best on every occasion. But ethical leaders are more consistent than others. If you will pardon a sports analogy, the ethical leader not only hits the October home run but also plays hard on the humid, late-August afternoon when the team is out of the pennant race and few fans are in the stands.

So far the focus has been on the behavior of individual leaders themselves: their ethical awareness, their attitudes, their choices, their relationships, the consistency and quality of their "own" work. The focus is important because no organization can be ethical without ethical leaders. But principals and superintendents are responsible for more than their individual behavior. They must also create and lead organizations that are themselves ethical in their design and operation. Schools and school districts are never value-neutral. They inevitably foster some values and slight or suppress others, and they often privilege some groups above others. How is the school organized and run? Who spends time with whom? Who makes what kinds of decisions? Who gets the resources that are needed and who goes without? What kind of behavior is rewarded? What kind is punished or discouraged? The answers to these and hundreds of similar questions determine the nature of the schools' ethical environment. A school that does not respect the worth of all its constituents is not an ethical school. A school that preaches equality and discriminates against the poor students is a decidedly unethical school. And so it goes. Leaders must attend not only to their own behavior but also to the effects of their behavior on the ethical quality of the institutions they serve.

This distinction between "microethics" (the leader's individual behavior) and "macroethics" (the ethical qualities of the organization, for which the leader is largely responsible) extends beyond the school. Schools and school systems are embedded in social, economic, and political contexts that have their own ethical (or unethical) properties. Sometimes injustices are obvious, as when poor children are not given the resources they need to do what we require of them. Sometimes the schools are caught in the conflicts between competing values, such as liberty (let families choose whatever schools they wish) versus equity (make sure that all students have equal educational opportunity, even if free family choice would produce other results). Educational leaders may not be able to eliminate such injustice or resolve such tensions. But at the very least, they should be aware of the ethical dimensions of such situations and should bring this awareness to bear on the matters within their purview. The individuals charged with education's heavy moral mission should be among the first to bring that mission to the fore.

One of an education leader's foremost macroethical obligations is to unite the organization's members behind a shared vision grounded in basic values. Of course, all organizations have purposes (or once had them), and effective leaders in any setting must help define a vision and bring people together behind it. But because of the moral nature of education, the tasks take on a moral dimension in the schools. As Sergiovanni (2001) says, "The school must move beyond concerns for goals and roles to the tasks of building purposes into its structure and embodying these purposes in everything that it does with the effect of transforming school members from neutral participants to committed followers. The embodiment of purpose and the development of the followership are inescapably moral." In this view, educational leadership is necessarily moral leadership as well.

Finally, being ethical means maintaining a lifelong habit of reflection on education's moral purpose and on one's own developing moral sensibilities. One is not born with moral certitudes, nor do the seeming certitudes of youth always survive lived experience. Some people find that secure moral guidance, while broadly helpful, must be fine-tuned to meet the specifics of the complex human situations we encounter. We need to draw continually on what we have learned, what we have come to feel, and what we have synthesized from our own experience if we are to understand ourselves and bring our wisdom to bear. In the crunch times, it is not to external sources that we turn for answers. We must look within. The ancient commandment was to "know thyself." This we can do only through experience and reflection. And as we reflect, we come to understand that the road to moral wisdom is not through applying abstract principles, but through raising honest questions.[12] Thus we develop as moral beings, shaping our identity through our actions and reflections upon them.

This poem was written by the celebrated poet May Sarton. I wish that I had written it.

In Time Like Air
Consider the mysterious salt;
In water it must disappear.
It has no self. It knows no fault.
Not even sight may apprehend it.
No one may gather it, or spend it.
It is dissolved, and everywhere.

But out of water into air,
It must resolve into a presence,
Precise and tangible and here.

Faultlessly pure, faultlessly white,
It crystallizes in our sight,
And has defined itself to essence.

What element dissolves the soul
So it may be both found and lost,
In what suspended as a whole?

What is the element so blest
That there identity can rest
As salt in the clear water cast?

Love, in its early transformation,
And only love may so design it
That the self flows in pure sensation
Is all dissolved and found at last
Without a future or a past,
And a whole life suspended in it.

The faultless crystal of detachment
Comes after, cannot be created
Without the first intense attachment.
Even the saints achieve this slowly;
For us, more human and less holy,
In time like air is essence stated.[13]

Becoming moral, in my view, is the opposite of restraint or detachment. It requires passionate engagement with other humans—"stepping in," as Gilligan would say, to all of life's confusion, heartbreak, and messiness, and losing oneself in something larger than one's self before the self can be defined. As I used to tell my students at Teachers College: "You are all on the way to becoming moral in this sense. I urge you not to hold back from commitment. You are the salt of the earth; you should savor life with your strength and your energy and your love. As time passes you will define yourselves in ways that will be good, for you and for those you touch." Remember what May Sarton says: "The faultless crystal of detachment / Comes after, cannot be created / Without the first intense attachment. / Even the saints achieve this slowly; / For us, more human and less holy, / In time like air is essence stated."[14]

Working was becoming harder and harder for me. My voice was getting softer and the computer was becoming more difficult. My left hand was contracting and I could see what was coming and it wasn't good. I knew my teaching was ending. I miss the students and the teaching every day.

Education Reform

We are embarked upon a nationwide effort to reform the schools right now. Or, to put it more precisely, we are embarked upon a nationwide effort to reform the schools again. The public schools have been constantly under attack. I can think of no time when they were not in some kind of crisis, from Sputnik and *Why Johnny Can't Read* to *A Nation At Risk* and the No Child Left Behind Act. Whatever their merits (and such cries of alarm are usually right in certain respects), their arguments provoke spirited discussion. Say "public schools" to a random sample of citizens: Ten to one what you will hear, from the left and the right, is a heap of scorn and derision laced by ridicule. It is rarely in vogue to say anything good about the schools.

Moreover, we are divided between those who want to dismantle the public school system and those who want to improve it, those who emphasize education as an individual property right and those who balance individual rights with the common good, those who regard teachers as the problem and those who see them as the solution. Caught in these ideological wars, politics eclipses pedagogy. School people struggle on, trying to make each day productive for their children and hoping the policy makers will listen to practitioners as well as to the political elite. I hope so, too. The new century has not yet decided how its children shall be educated, although there are signs that fundamental change is in the offing. Practitioners, I want you to be there when the decisions are being made, contributing knowledge about teaching and learning that only you have. Use it well. We are counting on you to enrich the quality of our children's education!

***

So much for context. Now for some practical advice. Obviously, I cannot in this forum give you a detailed plan for your school or school district, much less your state or the nation. Nor should I. None of us knows exactly what the schools of tomorrow should look like. Rather, I can give you several fundamental principles that apply to education reform at all levels. I can also make some suggestions for action that may set you on a desirable course and get you moving. But you will have to find the way. There is no road to reform. Reform is the road. Finding the way will not be easy. There is no silver bullet. There is no single condition or practice which if adopted could cure our ills; no deus ex machina to descend from on high to give us "the answer." Reforming education will be complex, demanding, frustrating, emotional, and consummately political. It will involve millions of people and billions of dollars, and it will affect everyone in intensely personal ways. Educational reform is how we decide what kind of children we want to have, and what kind of society we want to be.

Educational reform may be possible, given enough time, resources, and willpower. But there is no silver bullet. Furthermore, one size does not fit all. We are a large and diverse country with a large and diverse population, and what serves some well may serve others poorly. There is no best way to teach, no best way to learn, no best way to organize schools and schooling. A reformed system should be clear in its goals and flexible in its means. That principle applies to all levels of education, from a kindergarten classroom to the Oval Office. One size does not fit all. With these cautions in mind, what needs to be done if education is to be satisfactorily reformed? The measures outlined below are large, complex, and perhaps discouraging, but without their successful accomplishment we shall continue to tinker with trifles.

Develop Teachers' Capacity

The quality of a school cannot rise above the quality of its teachers. Teachers are central to any program of education reform. As our forebears have taught us, the essentials required for all teaching are threefold: the teacher, the pupil, and the book. Perhaps in this rapidly changing world we should substitute the word *computer* for the word *book*, but the fundamental dynamics are unchanged. Without a teacher there is no teaching. Without good teaching there is no good education. Without good education there can be no education reform. Our hierarchical but loosely-coupled schools and school systems give teachers formidable "power of the bottom over the top." (The phrase belongs to Harvard professor Richard Elmore.) Once the classroom door closes and the lesson begins, it is the teacher who decides what the curriculum will be, what instructional methods will be employed, and what materials will be used. It is the teachers who make (or fail to make) a motivating relationship with their classes. It is the teacher who decides what to do with the latest program imposed by the administration. And on it goes. Teachers have final discretionary authority at precisely the point where the rubber meets the road: in the classroom. If you want to improve the quality of teaching and learning, you must develop the capacity of teachers. Are teachers the problem or the solution? The answer is "yes." Yes, teachers are the problem, because they are ultimately responsible (along with parents and students) for our present shortcomings. And yes, they are the solution, because they are the people who must act if there is to be a solution at all.

I am confident in teachers' ability to find solutions. The teaching force in America represents a broad cross-section of the general public. Like an extended family, it consists of winners and losers, workers and shirkers, Democrats and Republicans. But they are virtually united in their concern for the children and for one another. Bring teachers into the tent and let them participate in educational decision making. You aren't going anywhere without them.

Most policy makers recognize the simple truth of these assertions. But they don't always act as if they did. Instead they have consigned the teacher-student-book triangle to a black box and ignored it. Charter schools, vouchers, merit pay, the business ethic, teacher tenure, and the No-Child-Left-Behind style of testing are all important, and each has had some success. But they are all input variables. Not one has transformed the schools. We need to open the black box and look inside. What is happening there? What are the teachers teaching? How are they teaching it? What are the pupils doing? Are they engaged with the teacher and the subject? What evidence of learning is there? For that matter, who is looking on? What do you see when you peek inside? As the great American philosopher Yogi Berra famously said, "You can observe a lot by just watching." Yogi was right, as usual.

Consider the School Quality Review program, an early '90s New York State Education initiative. Patterned on a similar program in England, the New York initiative convened teams of master teachers and parents to visit the schools. The visits were intense. The six to eight team members visited classes and talked with teachers and staff all day long for five consecutive days (typically Monday–Friday). In the evenings they worked on their end-of-week report. On Friday afternoon, once school was out, the team members, acting as "critical friends," met with the entire faculty and staff to discuss the team's findings, make recommendations, and plan a follow-up meeting at a suitable time. Most teachers (and principals) had never had a professional development experience of such intensity. It was very popular for three reasons: first, the evaluation was conducted by their peers. Second, all assertions concerning findings and recommendations were grounded in data. And finally, the data were chiefly obtained from classroom visits (twenty-five hours per team member multiplied by eight team members equals two hundred hours). The review helped teachers and administrators get to know their colleagues better and to see how their own work fit into the work of the school as a whole. We conducted these reviews in about a dozen schools to great acclaim. Unfortunately, when Governor Pataki was elected, he eliminated funding for this and similar programs, which many people viewed as a tragedy. It's apparent that the government and some educational leaders are still searching for a way to evaluate teachers, mostly through high-stakes testing. One could wish that within the evaluation process, professional growth assistance would be included.

School quality reviews are one small way to develop the capacity of teachers. In order to address the system as a whole we need a comprehensive, federal Marshall Plan for reeducating the nation's teaching force. The times, they are a-changing. We need teachers who are prepared to prepare our youth for life in the global village. Teachers should not only be able to effectively teach basic skills and core knowledge, they should be adept at teaching higher-order thinking skills such as problem defining and problem solving. They should know when and how to use deductive reasoning, and when and how to use inductive reasoning. They should be comfortable with both cognition and metacognition. And working collaboratively with their students (for we are all learners in the global village), they should explore the uses of new communications technologies, redesigning the system as we go.

Such an undertaking should not be isolated either, but should enlist the energies of government, business, higher education, the philanthropic communities, and the world of communications technologies as well as teachers' unions and other school representatives. Participating individuals and institutions should develop overlapping networks for training teachers in the new curriculum. Congress should enact legislation that provides broad guidance and support for these initiatives. Operating authority should be reserved for the states, who should collaborate with local school systems in the manner of the Elementary and Secondary Education Act (ESEA). One precedent for this is the National Defense Education Act (NDEA) of 1957, created when Russia's Sputnik ruled the skies. The act's goal was to improve the teaching of science, mathematics, and foreign languages. We can learn a lot by looking at that act's successes and failures.

There are a thousand more things we can do to develop teacher capacity, of course. I don't propose to write about them all. It would take me forever, and this is a memoir, not a treatise. But I hope I have convinced you of my core belief: that education reform depends on what teachers do, that teachers are both the problem and the solution, and that our teachers are smart enough and well-informed enough to reform the schools, provided we have the political will.

The Schools Can't Do It Alone

However, the schools can't do it alone. School is an important part of a child's life, but one cannot separate how children live from how they learn. The nature of a child's existence is often shaped by more powerful forces. Consider the effects of parents, other adults, churches, community-based organizations, television, the Internet, social media and computer games, friends, classmates, cliques and gangs, as well as the urgencies and confusions of puberty and adolescence. All of these influence the child and her or his attitude toward schooling. Young people coming through the schoolhouse doors each morning do not do so as students of the binomial theorem or irregular verbs. They are there as young people, fraught with all the blessings and all the misery of the human condition. Unless you meet their needs, or at least understand them, you won't get very far with your irregular verbs.

What can be done with these realities? Here are a few of the things we did in New York State during my eight years as commissioner of education. We increased the participation of parents in their children's education:

- by emphasizing its unparalleled importance,
- by making clear the various ways in which parents can help their children, in and out of school,
- by requiring schools and districts to form and maintain *A New Compact for Learning* committees of parents, teachers, and school administrators,
- by establishing centers in which parents could develop the skills and knowledge needed to become effective leaders,
- and by establishing after-school programs at which parents and children worked together to acquire computer literacy.

We also worked where possible to synchronize the services provided by educational, social, and health agencies throughout the state. Some schools were able to lodge health clinics in the schoolhouse itself, thus increasing student accessibility. This meant more glasses for students with eyesight problems, and more hearing aids for those who are hard of hearing. We established "community schools" that were open from 7:00 a.m. to 7:00 p.m. Eligible students could arrive before class to eat breakfast, socialize, and get themselves ready for the day. In the late afternoon, community-based organizations used the space to conduct recreational activities, arrange meetings with health and social service personnel, and provide voluntary homework help and tutoring services. The state funded about two-dozen such community schools on a pilot basis. It was gratifying to see how quickly the idea spread. It was also interesting to see where the idea spread: what was conceived as a remedy for inner-city problems proved to be as appropriate in rural areas and in the suburbs.

I have been telling you about some programs that were successful. Candor impels me to tell you about ideas that failed or never got off the ground. Here are two, one at each end of the K–12 spectrum. The first is education for four-year-old children, commonly called pre-K children. Well-conceived, well-run programs can be a wonderful experience for children at this age, as they joyfully explore the mysteries and miracles of the burgeoning life in and around them. Pre-K classes can also introduce children to school culture and help them acquire vocabulary that may go beyond the reaches of the home. For these and other reasons we took the position that all eligible children should have access to a publically-funded preschool program. However, our advocacy was limited. We never found the money or the time. The second matter, which we gave insufficient attention to, was the relative absence of bridges from high school to college and/or work. We don't handle this transition well in our country. There are some exceptions, but by and large eighteen-year-olds who graduate (or who don't graduate) from high school are left alone to find their way into the adult world. The result is a lot of unproductive drifting and a general lack of purpose.

Many European nations have incorporated apprenticeships, internships, and differentiated testing programs. They seem to do better. High school studies have more significance when they lead directly to college or a job. We need to get our high school, college, and business people together to examine the possibilities and plan the future. And we need to be sure to include the community colleges. They lead the way in this matter. There are a thousand ways in which collaborations can be structured to build bridges and promote education reform. There is no best way. Any good way will do, given adequate resources, time, and willpower.

One more item on this list of nonstarters: we never even mentioned a national youth service corps, such as a one- to two-year service internship required of all young people ages eighteen to twenty-two. Programs like this exist and are popular, but they all are voluntary.

What I am suggesting is a federal program enacted and managed locally, and a chance for young people to help older people. Have I gone crazy? Do I actually believe that some such required program is in the offing for all young people? No, and no. That's why I never mentioned it when I was commissioner. But if you don't believe me, just remember—some of you will be discussing the possibility within your lifetime!

Standards, Assessment, and Accountability

What are we trying to accomplish? How do we know if we are accomplishing it? Who is responsible for the results? These are the questions we must continuously ask as we pursue our course toward education reform. The following are some thoughts to keep in mind as we raise questions and seek answers. We need three kinds of standards. Content standards specify what should be taught and learned, performance standards set proficiency levels to be attained by students, and opportunity-to-learn standards indicate the extent to which necessary resources and conditions have been provided.

Content standards should be both broad and deep. They should be specific enough to provide guidance, but elastic enough to permit local variation and choice. Content standards should be developed by the states, with significant input by teachers. Standardized tests can provide useful information, but they should not be the only way we measure student progress. Students should have many ways in which to demonstrate their progress, including portfolios of their work, juried presentations, teacher judgment, and other forms of performance assessment. Again, standardized tests can provide useful information, but don't be seduced by their apparent accuracy and objectivity. The scores are subject to a wide range of inevitable error, a fact that should be kept in mind when making an assessment. Teacher judgment should be an important part of any child's assessment. Tests don't teach children, teachers do! Expand the idea of accountability. Just as our government holds students and teachers accountable for results, so our government itself should be held accountable for its share of the responsibility. In a democracy, government must be accountable to the people.

Take Your Time

Then we must be realistic about time. Schools are not fast-food establishments. They work in their slow, steady way season after season, year after year. Progress is not linear, as the No Child Left Behind Act seemed to depict. It is episodic, repetitious, and cumulative. Spurts of growth alternate with placid periods. We teach not only by instructing but by cultivating the strength that unfolds from within. The process takes time, and it cannot be hurried. Educating a group of children is like nurturing a garden, things need to be tended steadily and slowly, and it doesn't help to pull them up by the roots and measure them too often. I recently watched a public television program about migratory animals. It seems that every year millions of monarch butterflies leave their home in Mexico and fly north, heading for the cooler climes of the upper Midwest and Canada. The trip covers thousands of miles, and no one butterfly makes the whole distance. Instead they pause, lay eggs, and die. The larvae pupate, morph, take wing, and fly farther north. It takes three generations of butterflies to make the trip. We should embrace that wisdom. The schools will not reach their intended destination within the term of any single president or congressperson or state education commissioner. The policy clock and the pedagogical clock are not synchronized. Let's understand that, and quiet our rhetoric down. The question should not only be about whether the scores went up this year, it should be whether we have persisted in our journey, doing our part and noting progress, but respecting at all times the nature of butterflies and flight.

Beyond the Standards

Some people believe that the sole purpose of education is academic achievement, narrowly construed. High marks, good test scores, that's all that matters. No one denies the central importance of academic achievement in school. But it is not all that matters, not historically and not now. Schools are places where children come together to learn, and it turns out that the coming together is as important as the learning. Or rather, the coming together enables learning of a different kind. Children learn by establishing an identity among their peers, taking responsibility for their actions, learning to tolerate and maybe appreciate diversity, and balancing their own interests and desires with a sense of the common good. A good education helps children become competent, wise, and just. Competence alone is not enough. Our education reform efforts need to be informed by a deeper and more spacious conception of teaching and learning. Reducing the potential richness of a child's education to preparations for a standardized test score is a sad misunderstanding of the system's original intent. It may not seem so now, but a broader and deeper view will prevail. Remember the monarch butterflies.

EPILOGUE

Can we do these things? I think so. Will we do them? I am not sure. The political tides have been running against this kind of education, and relief is not yet clearly in sight. I suspect that in the end, much may depend on you, because it is a younger generation that will have to come to terms with these issues.

Meanwhile, I hope that these few ideas make sense to you, and that you will be influenced by them as you continue your own education and shape the education of others. I acknowledge that I have little faith in our plans and strategies for quickly bringing about the reforms we want. The changing world is too complex for linear thought to catch it. All schemes seem out of date, all solutions contextual and temporary.

But the outlook for the future is more promising. Harriet says I'm becoming a cynic, but she's only partly right. I'm a short-term cynic but a long-term idealist. I think that great things are possible if we remember who we are and what we're about. Over the past few years I have delighted in the growth of my youngest grandchildren, Colin and Dashiell. I have watched their squints disappear as they gradually opened their eyes, and their hands reach out until they could grasp. Soon their smiles of recognition began catching my breath. I've delighted watching them learn to sit up and turn over, and greet our moods with such resonance, and express such joy over each new taste or movement.

Whether it's a cliché or not, they are miracles. Aristotle was right: all men by nature desire to know. I ask myself, what do I want for Colin and Dash, and what by extension do I want for all children? I want them to grow strong in an environment blessed by love. I want them to discover their powers and use them fully. I want them to taste life and live it joyously. I want them to live decently and productively among others in their surroundings. I want them to understand all they are capable of understanding, give all they are capable of giving, live as fully as they are capable of living.

All this is a long way off from standardized test scores. But as I watch them grow while I decline, something I cannot name tells me that this is what life and education are about. Walt Whitman said it best:

> There was a child went forth every day;
> And the first object he look'd upon, that object he became;
> And that object became part of him for the day, or a certain part of the day,
> or for many years, or stretching cycles of years.[15]

You will know you are approaching education reform when each child goes forth each day to greet experience as old as time and as new as a tidal creek.

May the child in you go forth to spacious tomorrows, and may those you serve and lead look upon you and be touched by your loving spirit and useful hand.[16]

NOTES

INTRODUCTION

1. Thomas Sobol, "Teachers College Medal for Distinguished Service" (Teachers College, Columbia University Commencement, New York, NY, May 16, 2007).

CHAPTER 4: TEACHER

2. Gilbert Highet, *The Art of Teaching* (New York: Vintage Books, Random House, 1989).

3. Alfred North Whitehead, *The Aims of Education, and Other Essays* (New York: The Free Press, 1967).

4. Ibid., 14.

5. Robert Frost, "What Fifty Said," in *West Running Brook* (New York: Henry Holt, 1928).

CHAPTER 5: SCARSDALE

6. Robert N. Barger, "Summary of Lawrence Kohlberg's Stages of Moral Development" (University of Notre Dame, Notre Dame, IN, 2000), http://www.library.spscc.ctc.edu/electronicreserve/swanson/SummaryofLawrenceKohlberg.pdf.

7. Lawrence Kohlberg, "Moral Education: A Response to Thomas Sobol," in Educational Leadership.

8. Harvard University, "Harvard Class of 1953 Twenty-Fifth Anniversary Report" (Cambridge: Harvard University Printing Office, 1978)

CHAPTER 6: ALBANY

9. Thomas Sobol, "Revising the New York State Social Studies Curriculum," *Teachers College Record* 95, no. 2 (1993).

10. New York State Social Studies Review and Development

Committee, "One Nation, Many Peoples: A Declaration of Cultural Independence" (New York: New York Department of Education, June 1991).

11. Thomas Sobol, "Teachers College Medal for Distinguished Service" (Teachers College, Columbia University Commencement, New York, NY, May 16, 2007).

CHAPTER 5

12. Originally published in *The Principal Challenge: Leading and Managing Schools in an Era of Accountability*, edited by Marc Tucker & Judy Codding.

13. May Sarton, "In Time Like Air," New Yorker, May 12, 1956, 42.

14. Ibid., 42.

CHAPTER SEVEN: TEACHERS COLLEGE / COLUMBIA UNIVERSITY

15. Walt Whitman, "There Was A Child Went Forth," in *Walt Whitman's Leaves of Grass, 150th anniversary ed.* (1855; New York: Penguin Books, 2005), lines 1–3.

16. Thomas Sobol (remarks to the School Law Institute, Teachers College, Columbia University, New York, NY, July 17, 2003).

APPENDIX

A Sampling of Excerpts from Speeches and Articles

from A Time of Turning,
Scarsdale High School Graduation, 1978

(Speech originally printed in _The New York Times._)

Most students know me only as the perverse misanthrope who refuses to close the schools when it snows. In fact, the best story I know about a superintendent, a true story, by the way, concerns the first grade class whose teacher asked them to write down what their fathers did. One boy wrote, "My father is a doctor. He fixes people." A little girl said, "My father is an engineer. He builds bridges." And a third child put down, "My father is superintendent of schools. He doesn't do anything."

Ordinarily, when I have the opportunity to talk to a school audience about something other than the tax rate or enrollment projections, I talk about our educational program. I suppose I ought to talk about that again today, so let me do so quickly and be done with it. I hope that the courses of study and the lessons and the examinations and the homework assignments and all the classroom effort of the past thirteen years have prepared you well. I hope that you can read and write and reason clearly, that you know something of mathematics and the natural sciences. That you feel at home with literature and social science and the arts. I hope that you have learned how to ask good questions and that you have cultivated the discipline which the development of mental or physical or artistic talent requires. I hope you know about computer science and DNA and Shakespeare's genius and the fall of Rome and catastrophe theory and the twelve-tone scale—and if you don't have this knowledge and these skills, either because the school has failed you or because you have not been ready for them, I hope you will acquire them, for without them you are unlikely to continue learning in the future. "Where attainable knowledge could have changed the issue," says Mr. Whitehead, "ignorance has the guilt of vice." I wish you less destructive vices.

But that is not what I propose to talk about today. Now that all the exams have been graded and all the marks turned in, I'll tell you a secret (I suspect that many of you know it already). All this formal education that you've been involved in all these years, important as it surely is, is not the main thing that has been happening to you. The main thing is that you have been becoming a person. And we are here this afternoon not only to mark completion of your academic labors, which, after all, for most of you are far from done, but to celebrate your passage to a new stage of your emerging selves. It is a time of change and a time of turning. The identities and the relationships which you have now are about to alter, and what will come we can see only darkly. So it seems important here to seize this short moment in our lives and hold it firmly, even if we cannot fully understand it. The occasion is important, for all of us, and it must not slip unnoticed through our hands.

Many of us have been reading in these recent years about the stages of adult development. In books like Gail Sheehy's *Passages* and *The Seasons of a Man's Life*, as well as in the more scholarly work of people like Erik Erikson, we have read that just as children pass through predictable stages in the course of their physical and psychic development, so too adults throughout the course of their lives also pass through clear developmental stages. And, we are told, if the tasks of each stage are properly accomplished, each successive stage provides new opportunities for growth. Some of you may write this material off as the work of a bunch of middle-aged people trying to cheer themselves up. Some of you may find it a labored elaboration of what has long been intuitively known and better said. But I suspect that its popularity nowadays reflects a widespread interest in trying to understand our lives more fully, and in trying to extract meaning and purpose from the fundamental nature of our existence. So without any claim to special knowledge or wisdom, but promising to speak only that which I feel to be true, I would like to borrow from the spirit of this recent writing and say a word to each of the three generations here assembled—to you, the students; to your parents; and to the parents of your parents.

First, to the graduates.

You're leaving. I hope that you are fully aware of it....I hope that in your own way you can think back now and get some kind of good-bye. You will not have another chance....

For when you return to visit next fall, even as soon as next Thanksgiving, things will not be the same. The buildings will seem smaller and more crowded, the streets quiet and empty. Your home will still be your home but not quite in the same way, and your friends will be subtly different. And you, most of all, each of you will be different. Look around you now and hold these friends in memory, for never again, not even at your tenth or twenty-fifth reunions, will all of you be assembled again, and when some of you do meet it will be to weigh the changes. There is a sense in which home will always be with you, but much more surely is it so that, truly, you cannot go home again.

Ahead, you enter an exciting time. The span of years ahead of you is a time for energy and strength and testing, a time to separate from family, to explore possibilities, to assert your powers, to try on love and work for forms that fit you, to become autonomous adults. We need you to do so, for you are our collective vigor. And I would ask each of you in the wonderful but difficult years ahead to screw your courage to the sticking place, for each of you will have the chance to be much more than you are now. For those of you who have felt successful here in Scarsdale, whether academically or in other ways, I hope that the confidence you feel will be a base on which to build new strengths. And if you have felt less successful here, perhaps overshadowed in your own minds by others who seem brighter or stronger or more sure of themselves, I tell you that people do not stop growing at age eighteen. Look at any high school yearbook and compare it to the graduates twenty-five years later. What you will see is that some of the people you would expect to become mature, caring, and effective persons do so and some do not; some you would expect not, grow in surprising ways, and some do not. I do not fully know what it is that makes the difference. But I do know that if you retain an openness to your own capacities and to the possibilities of the life around you, if deep down you can think well of yourself and learn from your experiences, you may be much happier in the future than you sometimes feel now.

Now to the parents: it is for you a time of turning too. (I know because I am of your generation and have been here twice already, with more to come.) Most of the kids will be gone in the fall, and when they return you will be different with them too. Not that we exactly put them on a raft and push them out to sea: the financial ties, if nothing else, may be stronger than ever. But we know it is a time for letting go, for finding ways to show our love without controlling, for easing back while our children define themselves as different from us. For many of us, this separation of the young is very difficult. In men, I know, it is a sign of time's passage and our own mortality. I cannot know what it may be for women, but for those who have spent their adult lives nurturing the young who are about to leave, the separation, whether met with joy or sadness or plain relief, must be traumatic. And all of us must feel a certain rejection as our children adopt values and styles that are not ours.

But there are reasons to be glad. One is, that however different they may become, our children are also us and will be so always. Perhaps this is all genetic. I know it better from life and poetry. In *A Mass For The Dead*, William Gibson sees the behavior of the father and the grandfather in the child. Listen:

Across the garden a couple of two-legged miracles are growing up like grass, boys, running naked and beautiful under our apple trees....I see the older boy lose his temper at the sand pile, pounding with a rock on a toy derrick that is pigheaded, and I am bludgeoning an incorrigible spike ugly as a squashed snake into a plank of this studio going up, and my young father is grim over a talentless gadget he has brought home to my mother from a sidewalk pitchman, which ends up wrecked in our garbage pail, and it is some unknown grandfather of his whose fist is pounding sense with the rock into the toy derrick. The younger boy in a naked squat is maneuvering a chunk of old plank for a bulldozer, calmly making do, and in the garden my wife's father is erecting out of giant wind fallen limbs a fence that will withstand earthquakes, but is only for peas to climb, calmly making do (Gibson, 1968).

And there is another reason to be glad. Our generation, here at least, has opportunities for new life and experience without parallel, on such a scale, in history. We continue to care for our children, but unlike our parents or grandparents, we do not sacrifice our lives for them. We increasingly care for our aging parents, but by and large we have the means to do so without changing our circumstances. And meanwhile the Zeitgeist exhorts us to continue to grow, to change, to try new roles and define new structures for our lives. The women go to school, get jobs, publish; the men change jobs, release emotion, bake bread. No hunkering down to await old age for us; and if we can come to terms with our own limitations and illusions we can escape the tyranny of our early patterns and mature into lives which are good for all. The passage to another place may be stormy, but the journey is its own reward.

And finally, a word to the grandparents. I do not know your experience yet, so I shall not try to tell it to you. But I tell you a mystery; the young turn home toward you. This happened to me lately: I remember my father, when I was a child, home by streetcar from work in the rail yards, the smell of creosote on his boots and pants, on his breath beer, the huge workman's hands, the shortness of temper at whining voices in small rooms. I will transcend this, I dream. I remember my son in his childhood days, suburban lawns, forsythia and dogwood, the comfortable birthright of the middle class. I have given him at least this, I think. And now it is now, and we are at Sunday dinner with my son in college, at a credit-card restaurant high on a hill above the rail yards in downtown Worcester. We look down and he, who knew my father very little and my own childhood not at all, he tells us that often at nights when he cannot study he walks in the rail yards and visits the bars, he is drawn to the men, to their rough speech and smell, to a reality he cannot reach in his studies nor at home. And I chill to know that he will touch my father, though dead, in a way I was not able to.

I told you I have no special wisdom, so perhaps it is best that I should stop. Soon now, after the ceremony, we will leave this beautiful courtyard and go out into the afternoon and into the rest of our lives. Tonight and tomorrow may not seem much different to you. But I promise you, none of us here will ever be the same again.

This day, for all, is a time of turning. Let us rejoice and be glad in it.

from MESSING ABOUT IN BOATS: THE WATER RAT'S VIEW OF EDUCATIONAL EXCELLENCE

(First presented at the Westchester-Putnam School Boards Association
dinner meeting. Published in the *New York State School Boards
Association Journal*, September 1985.)

From the first "back-to-basics" outcries in the early 1970s through
the recent spate of national reports demanding "excellence" to the
commissioner's new regulations written following the adoption of
the Regents Action Plan, we have swallowed the assumption that the chief
purposes of education are academic, and academic chiefly in ways which
are readily measurable. We have raised our requirements, toughened our
standards, and improved our test scores. And so we have survived in the
prevailing climate. But in doing so we may have taken leave of sanity in the
way in which any single-minded fanatic may be said to be insane. We have
forgotten what education and schooling truly ought to be about....

I suggest to you that not all of education is academic and that not even
all of academic education is characterized by purposeful, structured, carefully monitored activity. Education involves the heart as well as the mind,
and learning entails play and risk-taking as well as ordered study.

Education and Growing Up

These are big thoughts. Instead of elaborating, I offer you the voice
of someone who holds a different vision of education, someone who re-
members what the world was like before we ate the poisoned grain. It is the
voice of the "Water Rat." Some of you may remember him, from Kenneth

Grahame's wonderful storybook *The Wind in the Willows*. What does the Water Rat have to say, in reply to this comment by his friend "Mole?"

"This has been a wonderful day!" said he as the Rat shoved off and took to the sculls again. "Do you know I've never been in a boat in all my life."

"What?" cried the Rat, openmouthed. "Never been in a—you never—well, I—what have you been doing, then?"

"Is it so nice as all that?" asked the Mole shyly, though he was quite prepared to believe it as he leaned back in his seat and surveyed the cushions the oars, the rowlocks, and all the fascinating fittings, and felt the boat sway lightly under him.

"Nice? It's the only thing," said the Water Rat solemnly as he leaped forward for his stroke. "Believe me, my young friend, there is nothing—absolutely nothing—half so much worth doing as simply messing about in boats. "Simply messing," he went on dreamily: "messing—about—in —boats; messing—"

"Look ahead, Rat!" cried the Mole suddenly.

It was too late. The boat struck the bank full tilt. The dreamer, the joyous oarsman, lay on his back at the bottom of the boat, his heels in the air.

"—about in boats—or with boats," the Rat went on composedly, picking himself up with a pleasant laugh. "In or out of 'em, it doesn't matter. Nothing seems really to matter, that's the charm of it. Whether you get away, or whether you don't; whether you arrive at your destination or whether you reach somewhere else, or whether you never get anywhere at all, you're always busy and you never do anything in particular; and when you've done it there's always something else to do, and you can do it if you like, but you'd much better not. Look here! If you've really nothing to do else on hand this morning, supposing we drop down the river together and have a long day of it?"

The mole waggled his toes from sheer happiness, spread his chest with a sigh of full contentment, and leaned back blissfully into the soft cushions. "What a day I'm having!" He said. "Let us start at once!"(Grahame, 1908).

In the Water Rat's view, education and growing up, which by the way go hand in hand, are more than a desperate preparation for the encounter in the admissions office. Not all educative experience can be planned and followed sequentially, nor can it be carefully measured. Much of what children learn that is valuable occurs when there is time for waggling the toes and messing about in boats.

Think about the child's experience in school. He or she enters the kindergarten year in September worried that he or she won't find the door again and nervous about where to go to the bathroom. Season after season passes—the fall leaves, the first snows, mud-time, the early heat and smell of summer, again and again. Friends are made, lost, betrayed, cherished, forgotten. There are holidays, birthdays, parties, picnics, field trips. There is laughing and fighting, tears flowing. There are endless summer vacations and annual fall renewals. By the time they leave in June of their senior year, they are sexually maturing, overconfident of their powers, and steeped in the values of the cultural mix in which they have thus far spent their lives—perhaps a quarter of the entire time allotted to them on earth. How do you summarize such a rich and seemingly endless life experience in a comprehensive assessment report?

The Water Rat knows what every child knows, that school is life, not just preparation for it; and he knows what every great scientist knows, that much learning and most discovery occurs through serendipity. (Not accident, by the way; scientists and schools can do better than that. Serendipity in the sense that the curiosity and the effort and the materials must be there, but the outcome turns out to be something else.) If the children are to grow, as we want them to grow, if they are to become full, thinking people with imagination, sensitivity, creativity, empathy, and the capacity to love, then there must be time for them to be children, to live life fully as children live life, in school as well as out.

There must be time for reading what isn't assigned, for doing an experiment you thought up for yourself, for painting something the way you imagine it instead of the way it looks. There must be time for playing ball or hanging out in the schoolyard before school, and for taking bike rides to nowhere on the way home. There must be time for taking the alarm clock apart without knowing how to put it back together, and for dawdling over the first red leaf of fall and for reading a story to a friend in the corner. There must be time for playing with a dollhouse with a friend even when they think you're too old, and there certainly must be time for daydreaming. As the body develops and consciousness grows, there must increasingly be time for sorting out your place in events and circumstances and relationships and for dealing with the central adolescent question which most of us never fully answer—for wondering who am I.

Identifying Goodness

By now you are probably thinking all this poetic talk is fine for someone from Scarsdale where nobody has to worry about money and everyone gets 800 on the SATs but down here in the trenches where we are....Wrong, on all counts. I live in the real world too, and by the way I am very proud of our students' achievement and very grateful to the families who send them to us so well motivated and prepared. Perhaps it takes someone from Scarsdale to acknowledge that academic achievement, as important as it is, is not our sole concern.

Perhaps it takes someone else entirely—in this case, a brilliant accomplished writer named Sara Lawrence Lightfoot, who teaches at the Harvard Graduate School of Education. She has published a wonderful new book called *The Good High School*.

Professor Lightfoot has written a series of six "portraits" of good high schools—two urban, two suburban, and two elite private schools. In clear, graceful prose, and with a disposition to be generous and to look for goodness, as well as to be critical, she captures the essence of each school as no recent writer within my experience. I urge you to read the book—I promise that you will find reflections of yourself there, even though no local school is among the six.

What is interesting about this highly acclaimed work from the perspective of this evening is what Professor Lightfoot identifies as "goodness." She writes:

> In good schools, students are treated with fearless and empathetic attention by adults. Teachers know individual students well and are knowledgeable about adolescence as a developmental period....Good schools exhibit coherent and sturdy authority structures which give support and legitimacy to the individual disciplinary gestures of teachers...good schools are also preoccupied with the rationale, coherence, and integrity of their academic curriculum...I do not see goodness as a reducible quality that is simply reflected in achievement scores, numbers of graduates attending college, literacy rates, or attendance records. I view each of these outcomes as significant...but each taken separately, or even added together, does not equal goodness in schools. "Goodness" is a much more complicated notion that refers to what some social scientists describe as the school's "ethos."

The consistent emphasis is on the wholeness of the experience, and upon the impact, which this wholeness makes upon the people, young and older, who attend and work in the school. And it is this definition of "goodness" as the wholeness of experience, which I should like to impress upon you.

Trustees of the Future

Educators are the trustees of our children's future. To a large degree the values that you reflect will be the values by which their young lives are shaped. As someone who serves a community renowned, justly or unjustly, for academic excellence, I ask you to remember that academic excellence is not all of education nor of schooling. What you hold in your hands is the gift of life itself, young, searching, straining, immanent life. Everything that happens to each child is a part of him or her, and it is your job to see that as much as possible of all that happens is good, even if you can't measure it.

from A VIEW FROM THE BRIDGE

WHAT DOES THE SCHOOL REFORM MOVEMENT MEAN FOR HIGHER EDUCATION?

(Published in *Trusteeship Magazine*, magazine of the Association of Governing Boards of Universities and Colleges, November/December 1993. Based on the author's remarks at the 1993 AGB National Conference.)

In the summer, when there's time, I hang out in the Adirondacks near a little town called Lake Luzerne. Leaving the town and going toward Hadley —just beyond Stone's Pharmacy and the bank, where they tell me the theater used to be—the road rises over a narrow bridge, crossing the still-narrow Hudson River just above its confluence, a couple of hundred yards downstream with the on-again, off-again, dam-controlled Sacandaga. If you get out of the car and hang over the railings of the bridge, as people do, you see a churning waterfall to the north and a succession of breaking rapids to the south until the river smooths out beyond the town and flows out of sight toward Corinth.

I am among those who, by virtue of long standing, have become familiar with the patterns of the water at this point. I know the slow, smooth surface of the water before it suddenly falls. I know the swirls and currents of each predictable eddy. I know the miniature backwashes in which sticks and leaves seem not to move. I know the turbulent frothing of water on stone as river meets river in the rocky gorge. But for all I know about the spin and rush of water within this narrow compass, I cannot tell you what you need to know about the river. I don't know where it starts, and my knowledge of where the water ends is largely limited to the hassle of getting across it or under it. I don't know much about the water, because whenever

I look at it, it looks about the same. And I am aware that each time I do look at it, the last time's water has long since vanished into the ocean or the sky.

Now it may be that I am so aware of the immediate swirls and eddies of my own profession that I read into them an importance they do not have. For decades, few of us have been satisfied with the results of elementary and secondary schooling, especially public schooling. Partly it is that we remember, or think we remember, a golden age that never was. After all, when I graduated from high school in the middle of the century I was among the one in two Americans who did so at that time. When my father graduated from high school during World War I, he was among one out of every four Americans. Today, we are graduating three out of four students and working very hard on the rest, trying to do what no nation ever has done—to bring virtually all of its young people to a level of genuine secondary school competence.

Even allowing for some rosy retrospection, however, most of us would agree that far too many of our young people today do not acquire in the schools the skills and knowledge they need to function effectively in our colleges or in the workplace. Even our best high school graduates lag behind their age-mates in other industrialized societies in their knowledge of mathematics, science, history, and their own and other languages.

For these reasons the schools perennially are being reformed. The nature of reform efforts differs from decade to decade to decade, but the visceral need to do things smarter and better remains constant. Some suggestions are better than others, but the chief reason that none of them have much impact is that, in reality, nobody pays much attention to them. The culture of the American school is wonderfully resistant to change. There is always a giant distance between the rhetoric of reform and the reality of the classroom on Monday morning.

We should not be surprised that this is so. Education does not take place in a vacuum, and people's heads are elsewhere. Nor should we despair that we have not accomplished much: we have educated not just an elite but, increasingly as this century has passed, all the children of all the people.

Meanwhile, however, dramatic developments on the world scene and in our own backyards have placed new demands upon us. These changes have rendered much of what we do obsolete, so the well-being of our society depends directly on our success in educating each and all of our children to new, high levels. And we cannot scale these heights just by working harder—by tinkering with the system of schooling we inherited from the 19th century. We must make fundamental changes in the ways we help all children learn. We need a new approach, one that harnesses the energies of local participants—teachers, parents, students, and a wide variety of others—with the resources and authority of the state. We need a program of "top-down support for bottom-up reform."

We need a new relationship between the state and the localities, one in which the state defines more precisely what is to be learned while local teachers, administrators, and boards of education have more freedom to decide how such learning is to occur. At the local level, teachers and parents must participate more fully in making decisions about school practice. And, of course, higher education is the final component.

How to Support Reform

For governing board members, the following six implications of the public-school reform movement are worth considering:

1. *Standards and Assessment.* The schools, government, business, and labor are in a ferment about standards and assessment. For better or worse, I predict that we shall see some form of national standards for student achievement and a national program of assessing progress toward those standards. We have the rudiments now (in the National Assessment of Educational Progress, for example), and people are lining up to expand upon them. The higher education community should

be a key player in the action, and boards can ensure this happens in several ways.

How is your admissions office incorporating the national standards movement into its plans? Each college should set standards for acceptable college-level work in its institution and hold all students to it. Yes, I know that some students may not be able to meet the mark initially, and I do not want to exclude them from the college experience. Continue to admit them, to coach and support them, to offer them second and third and eighth chances. But do not pretend with them that they are doing what they are not. Tell them when they are doing college-level work and when they are falling short.

If you have a school of education, is the curriculum taking into account the skills new teachers and advanced teachers will need to address standards? In New York, faculty and administration from both the State University of New York (SUNY) and the City University of New York (CUNY) system have worked with the state's Curriculum and Assessment Council to help spell out what students should learn in the schools, and they have brought their expertise to bear in improving assessment programs and practices. This collaboration has been fruitful and can be reproduced by other higher education institutions. One note of caution: avoid the urge to tell elementary and secondary teachers and administrators what they need to do to "shape up." Believe it or not, your faculty need schoolteachers' understanding of how children grow and learn as much as teachers need your faculty's scholarship.

2. *Teacher Training.* Two points worth emphasizing: first, teachers-in-training and teachers-in-service alike will need nourishing opportunities to learn new ways of doing things. They will need to learn about new curricula and assessment programs, new ways of working with parents and fellow practitioners, new uses of learning technology, and new ways to help the culturally different and those with disabilities. Any reform movement that ignores this huge task cannot be taken

seriously.

And second, teacher education is very much your business. It's fine to have the teacher-training colleges and departments, but remember that however effective or limited these institutions may be, they cannot do the job alone. In New York, more than half of our certified teachers do not complete an approved teacher-training program; they come in through the "back door," cobbling together the required education experiences after acquiring a baccalaureate of some kind.

3. *Achievement.* Maybe, given a few years to operate, the reforms now under way in K-12 education will produce high school graduates who can deconstruct Catullus, expound clearly upon chaos theory, and explain the multiplicative in verse without dropping a syllable. But don't bet on it. Don't dismantle your compensatory or remedial programs yet, and don't think you can trim your budgets of support services. The roots of our educational and cultural malaise run very deep and the soil in which they are buried is not the soil of education alone. It will be decades before we have so changed what we expect of ourselves and our young—and so changed what we are willing to do for ourselves and our young—that we will begin to approach the state of education we claim we want.

It will come, of that I am certain, barring some natural or man-made catastrophe. You can see it in the eyes and hear it in the voices of eager young people in thousands of elementary classrooms in all kinds of neighborhoods—classrooms where kids know they count, where they have identities and talents and even futures, where teachers are devoted and empathic and demanding and feel that they, too, are part of a learning enterprise. But the sober truth is that for the duration of most of your lives as trustees, you will not see dramatic change in the educational attainment of entering classes in your colleges and universities.

4. *Diversity.* Your students will be more diverse. Within a generation, one

of every three people will be what we persist in calling a "minority." The diversity will be not only a diversity of origins but a diversity of attitudes toward diversity. Many will continue to pursue the old idea of the melting pot, giving up form and substance like salt in water to be part of a uniform new America. But many will not: they will seek to retain the uniqueness of their backgrounds even as they participate in the economic and social mainstream.

Dealing with issues concerning diversity goes beyond revising your literary, historical, and artistic canons; it involves more than deciding how politically correct one should be or when it is correct not to be politically correct; it means more than showing *Malcolm X* at the campus cinema on Martin Luther King Jr. Day. For you as trustees, it will mean diversifying your board, faculty, and staff; making accommodations in scheduling and programming for people of different ages, backgrounds, and lifestyles; and providing living circumstances and a climate in which all can feel comfortable.

But most of all, it means coming to grips with how much you wish your institutions to change. What of the past, at all costs, must remain; what can and perhaps should be shucked off? These are vexing questions—questions to which there may be no best answers, questions that will test your intelligence and your wisdom and your humanity. I cannot help you. I tell you only that making the most of our diversity is a wonderful challenge that makes moral and economic sense.

5. *Technology.* We know that technology has transformed our lives and will continue to do so. Modern computer networking and interactive video can connect institutions—colleges and universities, schools, libraries, museums, businesses, work sites, research laboratories, and government agencies. Networks can make readily accessible to any user all our tests, studies, reports, databases, diagrams, pictures, audio messages and *Brandenburg* concerti....As you think about how best to use new technology in your institutions, do not limit yourself to

thinking about how it can help do more effectively what you already are doing. Think additionally about how can it change what you do.

6. *Value Added*. I'm sure you don't want to hear this one, but I predict that before too long, the "value added" questions will be raised even more insistently. Our students, their parents, and the government are all spending too much money on the experience we're offering not to want to know what they're receiving for it. It has happened in the schools, as it should have, and I have little doubt that it will happen in higher education as well.

If secondary schools succeed in changing their graduation standards from time served to skill and knowledge adequately demonstrated, and if colleges express more explicitly the content and performance standards needed for entry-level collegiate work, it will be a small trip to ask how far and in what way these entry-level skills have been raised by graduation. The problem is not merely one of politics; it rises to the level of a genuine intellectual and philosophical challenge. How do you measure growth in the open-ended pursuit of truth and beauty? What measures should be applied? Who should create them? And perhaps most difficult of all, how do you measure real learning without trivializing it?

Board members must begin to ask these questions. How much will we value diversity? How persistently will we strive for equity? How serious will we be about our new standards and pursuit of excellence in our lives as in our schools? How willing will we be to invest in our children's and grandchildren's future and in the quality of our own cultural and intellectual condition?

I do not know the answers to these questions. But whatever happens in government or in the economy, for the most part the answers will be hammered out piecemeal, one at a time, institution by institution, faculty by faculty, administration by administration, governing board by governing board. Get ready for these questions. They are just beyond the bend in the river.

(Great Neck, New York, 1996.)

Twenty-five years ago this month, on a sultry afternoon much like this, in this same park and on this same ground, with the same traffic noises in the background and the same smell of spring-grass in the air, the first students and teachers of the new Village School met to celebrate the graduation of their first senior class. Girls—they were "girls" in those days—wore long hair, long dresses, bare feet. Boys wore long pants, short pants, dress pants, dungarees, whatever. The music ran to flutes and tambourines. There were no long speeches, just personal good-byes from the juniors to the seniors. Love floated on the air like June-ripe pollen.

And then, before we were done, dark clouds seized the sky, a cold and sudden wind ripped the trees, lightning crackled, and the rain drove down. We ran to the nearby bandstand—Mitch, Amy, Andy, Rob, Arnie, Mal, David, Leslie, the other Amy, all the others—and scrunched together in the too-small space, dripping, shivering, hugging, laughing. It was a wonderful metaphor for the times: outside, the thunder of war and protest and seething violence; under the sheltering canopy, the warmth and love of the community we had created. We knew we had something special, then; but we did not know, could not have known, how special the Village School would become.

Beginnings are easier than continuings. The first spring planting, the runner's first mile, the start of the affair, the wedding ceremony— all of these are easier than what follows: the weeding, the watering, the persevering through heat and drought and grinding changes of season, the necessary self-denial, the quiet, patient husbandry. The genius of the Village School is not that it was first created, but that for a full generation students, teachers, and parents have tended a program whose essence is that it is annually recreated by its participants, and kept it fresh and new.

The Village School was conceived in passion in the heat of a cultural moment, but it has been sustained through love to become something universal. That is a stunning accomplishment. I am proud and happy to have been among those who huddled on the bandstand, but I have lived long enough to know that the real credit, the unsung glory, belongs to you who have, through patient, painful cultivation, sustained the act of ongoing creation for this quarter century. From as deep a place within myself as I can reach, I salute you.

from LEADERSHIP

(Original speech given at the Future School
Administrators Academy in 2002.)

L eadership is in, these days. Having had little success in reforming
the schools with a number of other silver bullets, many people
have decided that the problem that now needs fixing is the quality of leadership throughout our schools and school systems. This is certainly true of the business and not-for-profit funding communities. As the
Wallace-Reader's Digest Funds say in their LEADERS Count initiative,

> After nearly two decades of efforts at school reform, untold millions of
> children are still being left behind. What's increasingly clear is that a
> missing yet essential ingredient in those efforts has been quality lead-
> ership. In city after city, headlines tell the same story: principals and
> superintendents face a worsening crisis of neglect—in the quality of
> training and preparation they receive, and in the lack of support and
> even outright hostility from politicians, parents, and communities. Too
> often, we have created conditions that doom all but the most heroic
> leaders to failure. This, as districts in nearly every state face tough new
> learning standards, and as statistics suggest that nearly half the nation's
> superintendents will reach retirement age in the next five years, with no
> certainty that quality candidates are in the pipeline to replace them.

Today, I propose not to talk about these "pipeline" supply issues, nor
about the reasons why formal leadership positions have become more difficult to fill —although these are surely issues that demand our attention
at another time. Instead, I plan to talk a bit about the nature of leadership
itself. I think that our understanding of what leadership is, and where it

comes from, and how it works, has become much more sophisticated in recent years. My goal is to describe this new understanding in ways that you will readily recognize and subscribe to. If I succeed, I won't have told you anything you don't already know—I'll simply have put words to perceptions you have long had but rarely talk about. If I succeed, there will be no surprises—you will simply think "yes, of course, that is the way it is." (And that, by the way, is one form of leadership.)

Here, then, are ten characteristics about leadership. I think they apply universally. I am sure they apply to the world of schools and school districts.

Leadership is a function, not a trait.

Leadership is not an aspect of one's personality; it is whatever you do to provide direction, guidance, and support in a given situation. It is something one provides, not something one has. In the complex world of schools and school systems, there is need for leadership by many people in many areas at many levels of the organization. Nowadays people speak of "leaderful" organizations, meaning organizations in which the norm is that individuals in many different roles rise to the occasion and exercise the leadership the situation demands.

In this context, we should not confuse leadership with authority. In any organization, the quantum of positional authority is finite—there is only so much to go around. But the quantity of leadership is potentially infinite—there is as much leadership as people wish to step up and exercise. Again, leadership is a set of functions to be provided by multiple actors, not the personality trait of an individual.

Leadership is contextual.

The kind of leadership needed to help teachers master a new reading program is not the same kind of leadership needed to persuade the public to support a bond issue. The kind of leadership needed to revitalize a moribund organization is not the kind of leadership needed to keep a well-functioning institution healthy and productive. To be effective, leadership must vary with the circumstances and the time.

Because leadership is contextual, it should be shared by many people. No matter how small the organization, it is not for one person to provide whatever leadership is needed in each and every circumstance. No one can lead in all things. In a healthy organization, different individuals exercise leadership at different times, depending upon the needs and their abilities to meet them. Indeed, in a healthy organization a major part of the nominal leader's job is to develop leadership capacity in others and to provide opportunities for its exercise.

Leadership takes many forms.

There is no one right way. Effective leadership comes in many guises. Sometimes it provides direction; sometimes it provides support or understanding. Sometimes we see it all at once—in the way a specific problem is resolved, a specific situation handled. Sometimes we see it over time—in the way a relationship is maintained, a climate generated and nurtured, a sense of pride and purpose suffused throughout an organization. Sometimes we see it in big, dramatic moments (Rudy Giuliani on 9/11), and sometimes we see it in the quality of quiet, steady, day-to-day work and relationships. Sometimes, as with James O'Toole's Rushmoreans, we see it in life-long commitment to a set of worthy ideals. But be it sudden or prolonged, eloquent or mute, forceful or indirect, there is no one right way.

Leadership connects people with a shared vision.

No one is a leader without followers; and if you want followers in our democratic society, you can't just order people around—you must tap into a compelling vision shared by the people involved and make your objectives and their objectives the same. I get very uncomfortable when I hear some would-be educational leaders talk about "my vision," and how they are going to explain "my vision" to the troops and get them all to follow it. Not bloody likely. What leaders need to do is to articulate people's deeply felt values and hopes in such a way that they become a truly motivating force for all involved—"our vision." People will forgive an occasional misstep along the way if the long-range direction is clear and shared.

The leader understands and respects the work.

If you don't, you won't get very far. The leader doesn't have to be an expert—can't possibly be an expert—at all things. The orchestra conductor doesn't need to be an accomplished soloist on all instruments. But he or she had better have some feel for what it takes to play a violin or an oboe well, and some understanding of what it feels like to be a member of the group. In our case, if you want to provide leadership that supports effective teaching and learning, you'd better have a pretty good idea of what effective teaching and learning are all about, and a healthy respect for those able and skilled enough to make it happen. Ignorance will show you up, and disrespect may show you out.

The leader cares about the followers as well as the cause.

We often speak of education as being "a people business," and we would do well not to forget that truth. A would-be leader who doesn't care about his or her followers might get them to go along for a short time, but in the end, people will not follow someone they know doesn't care for them—just as children don't learn well from teachers they know don't care about them. Even more important, we need to respect people as the goals of education, not as the means to some other end. I tell students that "people are more important than the program." An effective leader cares more about the total well-being of his other followers than he or she does about whether the test scores have jiggled up or down a few points. And paradoxically, the caring leader is more apt to see the scores go up.

Effective leadership is moral.

Effective leadership is moral. Teaching and learning are themselves moral activities; providing leadership for those who teach and learn raises the moral stakes. Commenting about the research literature on leadership, Tom Sergiovanni writes:

Why has the yield in practice been so dismal, given all our efforts? I believe there are two reasons for the failure of leadership. First, we have come to view leadership as behavior rather than action, as something psychological rather than spiritual, as having to do with persons rather than ideas. Second, in trying to understand what drives leadership, we have overemphasized bureaucratic, psychological, and technical-rational authority, seriously neglecting professional and moral authority....The result has been a leadership literature that borders on vacuity and a leadership practice that is not leadership at all.

I can tell you from first-hand experience that many of our students hunger for consideration of the moral nature of their work. We would do well to heed them, and not let our technical-rational training obscure needs and motives we know in our gut to be deep and powerful.

Effective leadership is about ideas.

We have said that leadership is moral. It is also about ideas. I find James O'Toole particularly persuasive on this point. He writes:

> Leadership, in the final analysis, is not about style but about ideas. Ultimately, it is ideas that motivate followers, and concepts powerful enough to energize people are typically broad, transcendent, even "philosophical" in nature...Learning to lead is thus not simply a matter of style, of how-to, of following some recipe, or even of mastering "the vision thing." Instead, leadership is about ideas and values. It is about understanding the differing and conflicting needs of followers. And it is about energizing followers to pursue a better end state (goal) than they had thought possible. It is about creating a values-based umbrella large enough to accommodate the various interests of followers, but focused enough to direct all their energies in pursuit of a common good.

We all know that in our business—the education and development of all society's children—there is more at stake than higher test scores. If we are to be leaders, we must define for ourselves what these ideas and values are, make them plain to all our audiences, and show their connections to the deepest aspirations of the people whom we serve.

Leadership begins with ourselves.

Effective leadership begins with ourselves. People who think that leadership consists of telling others what to do have spent too much time in the old army or in the State Education Department....As Mahatma Gandhi put it, "We must be the change we want to see in the world."

In colloquial terms, we must walk the talk. Or, to use one last quotation, here are Peter Senge's words: "The core leadership strategy is simple: be a model. Commit yourself to your own personal mastery."

Leadership creates a lasting culture.

The effective leader creates a culture that embodies these understandings and that is strong enough to survive his or her departure. Time and mortality outrun us all. We cannot hold our jobs forever. If the leadership we provide has been truly effective, we will leave a legacy in others: the capacity and will to exercise leadership on their own, the sense that doing so is right and proper. Shared leadership, focused on children's learning and development, will have become "the way we do things around here." The body, alas, decays. Ideas and principles, if they take root, can last forever.

ACKNOWLEDGMENTS

My thanks to Victor J. Goldberg, a generous, astute man, who thirteen years ago suggested we develop our respective oral histories. We did so, and my story gave birth to both this book and a lasting personal friendship. I am grateful to him for his steadfastness, sense of humor, and loyalty. Carol Choye, for her gift of friendship and all kinds of help, not to mention inordinate amounts of lemonade and cookies. Clare B. Hickey, whose computer skills and intelligence were invaluable in the book's early stages. My brother Walter Sobol, for his visits, childhood memories, suggestions, and laughter. Dr. Carl Weber, who saved my life. Rev. Bill Johnson, my favorite minister, theologian, and Major League Baseball player, who helped me to understand the publishing process. Averil Gordon and Angela Carter, who keep me as healthy as possible. Anne Campbell who helped me contact people who could find material I wanted at the State Education Department. Tom Dunn and Nellie Perez, for finding an ancient scurrilous article about me from the *New York Post*. Dr. Donald Kaye, who told his sister, my wife, to find a project for me. Karen Van Den Heuvel, a brilliant assistive technologist who smiles all the time, and who taught me to write using my computer with my one useful finger. Manuel Velazquez, my wise, skillful, and reliable friend, who is always here when I need him. Samantha Post, who organized my papers, speeches, and articles. Elizabeth Evans, for her interest in my book. Kate Whittemore, whose knowledge of the Albany scene has been of help to Harriet's research for *My Life in School*, and has evoked in me cherished memories of working together with Kate in Albany. Jeff Langsam, for providing excellent technical and purchasing assistance. Jenny Langsam, for being available to copyedit at a moment's notice. Gosia Kolb, a resourceful and loving friend, who chased down articles and images at Teachers College. Will Wyatt, who inspired me, but told me what to leave out of the book. Dennis McNitt, who scanned, organized, and sent all the images to my editor, Nadxi, and made himself available for emergency computer assistance. Jill Iscol and Peter Cookson, who generously recommended to us the wonderful publicist/agent, Lisa Weinert, and designer, Nadxieli Nieto Hall. Marya Levenson and all the Public Schools For Tomorrow people who keep me up-to-date with the education world. Readers, friends, helpers, and critiquers, Peter Cookson, Robert Di Yanni, Chuck Fowler, Renee Gargano, Jane Gerber, Andy Hawley, Nona Lyons, Joan Mark, Bill Miller, Joy Moser, Norma Myers, Gerard Pelisson, Laura Strauss, Betty Pforzheimer, Kathy, Joe, and John Plummer, Maj-Britt and Michael Rosenbaum, Susan Sagor, Elaine Schroeder, Laura Strauss, Sue Taylor, Joan Weber, and all the other readers, visitors, and e-mailers who have kept me connected to the world outside. Harriet: her intelligence, intuition, and persistence are relentless. She uses her remarkable teaching, writing, and managerial skills to find ways to help me in matters great and small. Without Harriet, there would be no project, no book, no me.

Tom Sobol is a graduate of Harvard College and the Harvard School of Education. He received his doctorate from Teachers College, Columbia University. He was Scarsdale Superintendent of Schools for sixteen years and New York State Commissioner of Education for eight years. After retiring from the commissionership, he became the first Christian A. Johnson Professor of Outstanding Educational Practice at Teachers College, Columbia University. He is the co-author of Your Child in School K-2 and Your Child of School 3-5 and has published numerous articles. He lives with his wife and their black lab in Scarsdale, New York.

Made in the USA
San Bernardino, CA
26 July 2015